California's Gabrielino Indians

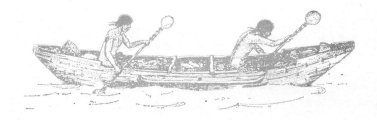

By

BERNICE EASTMAN JOHNSTON

SOUTHWEST MUSEUM
LOS ANGELES, CALIFORNIA
1962

FREDERICK WEBB HODGE
ANNIVERSARY PUBLICATION FUND

VOLUME VIII

DEDICATED TO THE MEMORY OF

JOHN PEABODY HARRINGTON
(1884-1961)
ARCHEOLOGIST, ETHNOLOGIST AND LINGUIST

00147 8180

Foreword

BY THE END OF THIS YEAR, according to statisticians, California will surpass New York by becoming the most populous state in the Union. Should this not prove to be the case, certainly by the end of this decade the Golden State will be able to boast of having the greatest population in the United States of America. To many people this might seem quite extraordinary. However, in view of the fact that ethnologists believe the area now comprising the State of California once supported the largest aboriginal population in North America, present statistics would indicate that population problems are "par for the course" of California history.

Favorable geography, climate and abundant nature made living conditions in what is now Southern California as attractive to prehistoric Americans as it is to today's inhabitants. Anthropologists may not be able to prove that ancient Indians were drawn to Southern California, as peoples have been in recent times, but they do know there were movements and migrations of peoples in California's primitive past.

Not that shifts in population are "as old as the California hills," but it is important to realize that primitive man was as much a searcher after a better life, or the better things of life, as his modern counterpart. Along the same shores, now dotted with highly developed harbors and cities, over the same trails now transformed into freeways, in the same valleys and on the same mountains, modern man has followed and built on an ancient life. The nearness of California's primitive past — the quick pace of history here — dramatize the great change that has taken place on the shores of the Pacific in little more than a hundred years. Few areas in the world have witnessed such a miracle of growth.

The Gabrielino Indians of Southern California have naturally always been of great interest to the Southwest Museum staff and members. Since the Museum's founding in 1907, anthropologists, artists, historians and writers all over the world have called upon it for information regarding these interesting aborigines. Indeed, the first archeological fieldwork done by the Museum was among Gabrielino sites. Some of the first ethnological material in the Museum's collection was representative of these people. The Museum's research library began with a gift of books and manuscripts from its founder, Charles Fletcher Lummis, many of which concerned the Gabrielinos and their aboriginal neighbors.

Of all the anthropologists who have studied the Indians of California, none was more distinguished than John Peabody Harrington of the Smithsonian Institution. After a lifetime in the field of American ethnology, much of which was spent in studying the Indians of Southern California, Dr. Harrington wrote that "a book on the Gabrielino Indians deserves to be printed and I hope that the Southwest Museum will do it."

Coming from one of the great authorities on these people, the Museum took pride in receiving his praise of Mrs. Bernice Eastman Johnston's inspiring work on the Gabrielinos which ran serially in *The Masterkey*. With his preface and the material provided by the notes from his early Gabrielino informants, this work fills an important gap in our knowledge of California's past.

The long, warm friendship of Dr. Harrington with Charles F. Lummis, the Museum's founder, and Dr. Frederick Webb Hodge, its outstanding director for so many years, is an inspiring chapter in the Museum's history. Dr.

John Peabody Harrington died in his 78th year, October 21, 1961. His preface to this work is among the last of his long list of scholarly writings. His contribution to American ethnology will never be forgotten. It is the hope of the Southwest Museum that this work on the Gabrielino Indians of California will serve as a tribute to him and all he did to preserve the record of a remarkable primitive people. The book is the culmination of endless hours devoted to research in many publications and manuscripts, as well as field trips to relocate old sites and interview knowledgeable persons.

It is no easy task to winnow the records of a vanished people. The Gabrielinos, like so many Indian tribes who owe their extermination to the whites, had few champions among the new settlers. But the civilization which engulfed them did have a few enlightened settlers, like Hugo Reid, whose letters to the *Los Angeles Star* awakened some interest in them and their plight. This famous pioneer, fortunately, was an exception to the casual disregard for the American Indian and his culture as practiced by his contemporaries.

The late Dr. Alfred Kroeber, a long-time friend and advisor to the Southwest Museum, contributed much to our knowledge of the Indians of California. His many studies concerning the early inhabitants of the southern part of the state have assisted greatly in the preparation of Mrs. Johnston's work.

Dr. Gerald Smith, director of the San Bernardino County Museum, and Don Meadows, of Santa Ana, contributed notes from their firsthand archeological studies. Great encouragement for this project was given by W. W. Robinson, California historian. The information he supplied on tracts of Mission land given to the Indians was invaluable.

In tracing ancient waterways in the Gabrielino area, the engineers of the Department of Water and Power, City of Los Angeles, and the Engineering Department of the City of Pasadena, were most helpful. Among many others Dr. Arthur Woodward, formerly of the University of Southern California, contributed information. Allen Welts, recent preparator of the Southwest Museum, drew the maps which accompany this book, as well as some of the illustrations. One of the Museum's archeological advisors, Hasso von Winning, contributed his talent by drawing the vignettes for chapter headings. Thomas Workman Temple II provided important items from the early California records in the Bancroft Library.

Inspiration came from the interest and enthusiasm of hundreds of teachers and thousands of school children throughout Southern California who have sought information at the Museum and elsewhere about the Gabrielino Indians. For years they have needed a handbook covering all aspects of these interesting Indian people to aid them in their studies.

It is hoped that in the very near future this work will be augmented by a book written only for young people. Considering all aspects of the tremendous growth of the City and County of Los Angeles, with its challenging population explosion, the proposed juvenile publication, "When Only Indians Lived in Los Angeles," will be a welcome addition to the literature for children.

Meanwhile, this long overdue work, "California's Gabrielino Indians," is finally able to make its debut because of the help of all of the aforementioned persons and institutions, along with that of the devoted members of the Museum's staff. In the very best spirit of the Southwest Museum, always desirous of serving the people, this work is offered to the public as Hodge Fund Publication No. VIII.

CARL S. DENTZEL
Director

Southwest Museum
Los Angeles, California
July, 1962

Preface

By John P. Harrington

THIS IS A THOROUGH, WELL-WRITTEN BOOK, which elicits the admiration of all of us. The material first appeared as a series of articles in *The Masterkey*, issues of November-December, 1955 to January-February, 1958. It tells about the Gabrielino Indians, former inhabitants of the coastal region of Los Angeles County, the northwest portion of Orange County and offlying islands. These people take their name from the famous San Gabriel Mission, seven miles northeast of the center of Los Angeles.

Archeologists, ethnologists and historians will alike find the book intensely interesting and filling a long-felt want, for it tells not only what is known of the native culture but also gives all the Indian names of places and connects many of these with known archeological sites. The book deals oftentimes with the very outposts of human knowledge and presents throughout in well-written form what can be snatched, even at this late date, from the fading memories of survivors. A good and thoroughly based book on the Indians of Los Angeles has at last been produced!

Especially the Southwest Museum, child and creation of Charles Fletcher Lummis, should be proud in having produced this book. It is such a work as Mr. Lummis would have been intensely interested in. I can vouch for this. I was at the Southwest Museum during its finishing and during the period of its opening and am proud to say that I had quite a friendship with Mr. Lummis. I lived in the Museum's tower and used sometimes to go down to Mr. Lummis's house.

He had become interested in ethnology when he lived at Isleta, New Mexico, and loved especially anything that dealt with the ethnology, history or archeology of Los Angeles County. He was a man of real ability in several distinct fields and it was indeed a privilege to know him. When he knew that he had to die, he went into his library and took down my book on The Ethnogeography of the Tewa Indians and charged me to carry on. He was one in his own words:

> ". . . forever young,
> Heart aflame with songs unsung,
> In his three score years and ten
> Lived the lives of many men."

Such a book as Mrs. Johnston has produced would have interested him greatly. He knew the county and liked to learn of olden times. Lummis enjoyed picturing vanished things.

The Gabrielino had four different dialects: Gabrielino proper, Fernandeño, Santa Catalina Island language, San Nicolas Island language. Perhaps the language of San Clemente Island was related to that of Santa Catalina Island. The archeology of San Nicolas Island is related to that of Santa Catalina Island and San Clemente Island. Of the San Nicolas Island language we have only four words.

The first "letter" of the series of "letters" published by Hugo Reid in the *Los Angeles Star* in 1852 lists 28 "lodges or rancherias," but Nos. 13 and 28 are islands and not villages. The number of place names included in the present work is vastly greater, and sometimes a new name is located with absolute certainty.

Special attention is here called to the unique value of Part 5, where a map is given. San Pedro and Los Angeles Harbor are shown to be at the mouth of Old River San Gabriel.

We should be truly thankful to Mrs. Johnston for this splendid, thorough and well-written work.

Contents

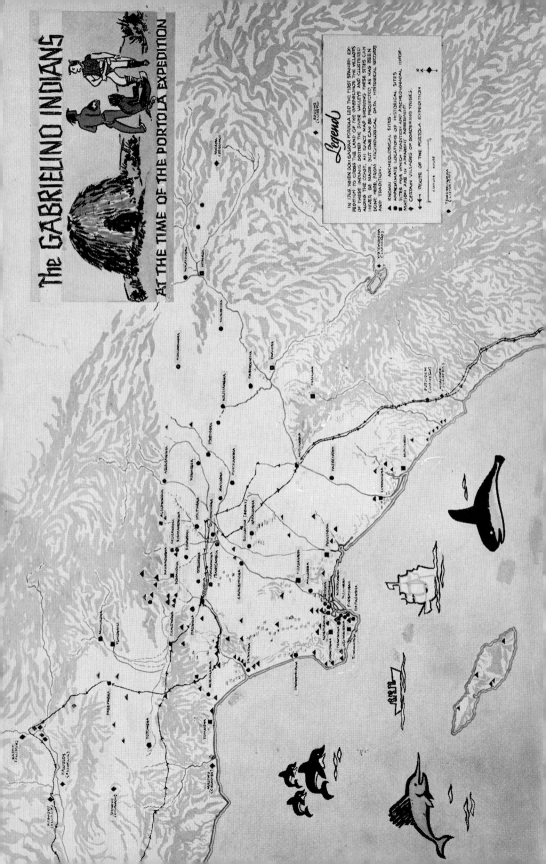

California's Gabrielino Indians

By BERNICE EASTMAN JOHNSTON

Introduction

HAVE you ever heard of Kawengna, Asuksangna or Yangna? The first two may contain vaguely familiar sounds and, if you should happen to be the parent of a child in the Los Angeles City Schools, you are no doubt well informed about Yangna, that small aggregation of round, symmetrical huts, fashioned of tules, which was the predecessor of the modern city.

Though not to be found in atlas or encyclopædia, these three and many others were villages of the tribe of Indians which Portola, the Spanish Pathfinder, found in happy possession of the coastal plain from Aliso

Creek in Orange county to a point somewhere between Topanga and Malibu, California. Kroeber estimates that in 1770 the population was about 5000. Today only an anonymous handful remains, and these few have little first-hand information as to the language or customs of their ancestors.

The time has long gone by when it would have been possible to make an exact map showing the locations of these villages, and our sources of information are now largely crystallized. In all writing on the American Indians, even of those groups living in historic time, a great deal must be labeled as unknown or uncertain, but in the case of the vanished Gabrielinos even the tribal name by which they are designated comes from a time, late in their history, when they were attached to the Mission San Gabriel Arcángel as satellites of a culture and a religion literally as remote to them as west is to east.

No one knows how long it took the Asiatics who became the American Indians to fan out across the new continents into the patterns of occupancy which existed when the first Europeans appeared. The Uto-Aztecan linguistic stock spread so far in its age-long migrations that between some divisions there remains only the whisper of a relationship, and in the Shoshonean branches of it, to which the Gabrielinos belonged, are included such distant cousins as the buffalo-hunting Comanche of the Great Plains and the peace-loving Hopi farmers of the mesa pueblos in Arizona.

These Shoshoneans were not the first Indians to find a homeland on Southern California's coastal plains. Their arrival seems to have been comparatively late and to have driven a great wedge between tribes of another language stock, the Hokan. There is nothing to show exactly when this change of occupancy took place or that the newcomers displaced the Hokan-speaking tribes by force or even found them in possession. Yet Shoshoneans occupied, at last, an immense wedge of land tapering from an expanse of 600 miles on the Nevada border to a mere 100 miles of seacoast, where they stood between the Yuman tribes of the southern border counties and an immense patchwork of diversified groups to the north of the Tehachapi, the Tejon and the Santa Susana watershed.

Legends are not safe substitutes for history, but it is interesting to note that, as if in memory of the vast empty lands once traversed, a feeling of awe colors a portion of the creation legend in which it is said that the earth grew ever to the southward and the people followed. It is quite certain that these Shoshoneans drifted across from the Great Basin by way of the mountain passes. Legend assigns a camp of the "first people" to a place in the Cajon Pass, at a time when "the earth was still soft." No warfare is mentioned, only naked, cold and lonely people, led by a wise "captain" southward into an ever-expanding land.

Somewhere in their former wanderings these primitive folk had been in touch with the earliest and as yet undeveloped Pueblo cultures. What little they brought into California with them contained but faint vestiges of the cultural seeds which were later to flower in the Southwest. They, themselves, were never to attain the artistic eminence of their fellow Shoshoneans, the Hopi, yet they were not without a special gift of their own which would develop along the lines of its own genius.

In Arizona and New Mexico archeologists have been able to satisfy a thirst for specific dates through pottery and tree-ring studies, among other methods, but these are of no use here. The Gabrielinos, in particular, made no pottery before Mission times, preferring the fine cooking pots of steatite, or soapstone, from Santa Catalina Island. The willow frameworks that formed the skeletons of their tule-thatched huts, which the Spanish were to call "jacales," long ago were burned or withered to dust.

Estimating the time necessary for languages to split off from the common tongue and to become obviously separate dialects, Kroeber postulated four periods, during the first of which the Hokan-speaking tribes lived almost undisturbed. After that, possibly about 500 B.C., other tribes began filtering in, gradually forming the great northern "patchwork" and the Shoshonean

Gabrielino handiwork: stone knife with wood handle, bone harpoon, steatite bowl, shell fishhook, stone whale effigy and boat-shaped stone bowl.

"wedge" so noticeable on Kroeber's map of the California Indians. By about 500 A.D. the cultures of all these tribes had begun to differentiate, to take on special characteristics in social and political structure and in religious formations. In the fourth period, which is placed in this tentative scheme as that following 1200 A.D., these cultures crystallized into the forms noted by the Spanish during their explorations.

Long before the coming of the Hokan-speaking tribes, back in still deeper and more shadowy reaches of time, yet other peoples had explored or settled here, leaving faint traces which form exceedingly dusty clues with which the archeologists must work in an effort further to clarify the story of early man in California. Even the comparatively recent Gabrielinos must be studied in this way. For example, in an excavation by the Southwest Museum of a known Fernandeño site at Big Tujunga Wash, pottery fragments were found that were identified as those of one vessel of Hohokam ware of the 7th, 8th, or 9th century, A.D. Such an item from southern Arizona indicates contact, possibly through the Mohave Indians who were enterprising traders, and provides a date to show that by the time this item reached them the coastal Shoshoneans were well established, with a definite culture based on long occupancy.

In our own time, when steam-shovel, bulldozer and paving machine are busily changing the face of the once Gabrielino earth, the old landmarks of these early Shoshoneans are rapidly being destroyed; indeed, even the fact of the existence of these Indians is almost forgotten. Yet occasionally a broken metate, a mortar, an arrowhead, or even a rare skeleton, disturbed in its rest by a mechanical ditch-digger, serve as reminders. Sometimes also an imaginative home-owner allows his thoughts to dwell for a moment on what his land looked like in Spanish times or when it was occupied by the quiet brown folk of the chaparral, long before the white man came.

It is for this home-owner, as well as for the student, that this review of available information about the Gabrielinos and their villages is undertaken. The culture of the metropolis which is now building on the coastal plain should send its roots deep into the true aboriginal soil.

In Shoshonean times, as in our own, many trails converged at a spot near the present Union Station in Los Angeles. It might be logical to begin a study of Indian place names here, but since the small village of Yangna, which was not far from that focal point, embodies in itself the climax of the Gabrielino story, it seems better to follow another scheme and give precedence to the borderlands.

The
Northwestern
Borderland

Most of the neighbors of the Gabrielinos were Shoshoneans like themselves, speaking dialects that showed separations of shorter or longer periods. The Paiute and related tribes which had remained in the desert, and the Cahuilla and the Luiseños, covering desert and mountain areas over to a coastal strip by San Luis Rey, were less closely related than were the Juaneños, who became attached to Mission San Juan Capistrano. Using dialects so similar to that of the Gabrielinos that they are classified with them as one people were the Fernandeños, who lived on the upper reaches of the Los Angeles River, and the islanders of Santa Catalina and perhaps of San Clemente.

Very little of the fertile lowlands was left to those Shoshoneans who are classified under the general heading of Serranos, or "mountaineers." The upper Santa Clara Valley, the Tehachapi and the Tejon, the San Gabriel Mountains and the San Bernardinos belonged to various bands of Serranos. Beyond these places only the Kern River Valley was held by Shoshoneans and these were independent migrants much modified by long contact with their neighbors of the San Joaquin Valley and the Sierra.

In Ventura and Santa Barbara counties lived a Hokan-speaking people whom we call the Chumash. Long separated from the tribes of the southern border counties and those other Hokans, the Yuma and Mohave bands, the Chumash had made in later periods a striking development along technological lines.

In 1769 Father Crespi, the diarist of the Portola expedition, wrote of them, "They are of good figure and disposition, active, industrious, and inventive. They have surprising skill and ability in the construction of their canoes, which are made of good pine planks, well-joined and of a graceful shape, with two prows. They handle them with equal skill. Three or four men go out into the open sea in them to fish, and they hold as many as ten men. They use long oars with two blades, and row with indescribable lightness and speed."

So important were these canoes and other items originated by these inventive people that they were copied by the Shoshoneans, with the result that the material culture of these tribes, for an indefinite distance down the coast and on the Channel Islands, is practically one and the same. For this reason most modern scientists disregard the tribal names, which are arbitrary anyway, and even the language distinction, and lump the whole scheme of living which prevailed in this channel area at the time of the advent of the Spanish under the heading of "Canaliño Culture."

We hear of the coastal Gabrielinos taking to sea in the plank boats, mariners in this Canaliño tradition. Hard work and great skill were used in the making of these fine craft, with their two prows, and sometimes wing-boards as well. Driftwood logs had to be split into planks with wedges made of bone or antler, and planed with stone scrapers. Drills of stone cut and reamed the holes through which strong cords of fiber were laced. It is said that the planks were buried in wet sand with fires built above them in order to make it possible to bend them into place. Deerhide thongs were never used as lacings since these would have stretched, letting in the sea at every joint. As it was, even after the most thorough calking with asphalt it was necessary on all extended voyages to take along a youth or two whose duty it was to bail out the inevitable and sometimes formidable seepage. These boats ranged from 12 to 16 feet in length. Having no skeleton, they depended on the keel for strength.

Another boat in general use would seem fit only for the most placid lagoon, although it actually did brave the surf out into the open sea where, bearing one or two fishermen, it would be, as one explorer described it, lost to view for many hours. This was a canoe-shaped raft, or balsa, made of the rushes the Spanish were to call "tules." It took experience to know just when to harvest these, as at a certain stage they were best suited to forestall the nemesis of such a craft, water-logging. Three long, shaped bundles of the rushes were lashed together to form the rather bulky but not at all clumsy shallop. Great care was taken to beach and to shelter them from rain, in order to prolong their usefulness.

If we continue, however, with the task of finding the geographic line between the Gabrielinos and their neighbors we must return to the linguistic classification. Early in our own century an old Gabrielino used this method to outline a small segment of this border when he said, "Beyond El Triunfo and Las Virgenes the Indians spoke a strange language."

On a map of the Santa Monica Mountains are to be found these names, coming down to us from Spanish times. To visit this area is to step back into an earlier day. The ancient oaks to which the Indians came for their staple food, the acorn, still dot the gentler slopes and where the canyons narrow are to be found little reminders of the marshes where the tules once grew in great profusion.

With the hundred or more known village sites in Ventura and Santa Barbara counties we are not concerned, but only with those of the border. Malibu was definitely Chumash, while at Topanga we are on Ga-

brielino soil. Farther inland were villages of Serranos
for which only Chumash names have been recorded.
Two of these were *Kamulos* and *Kash-tic*, readily recognizable as the modern Camulos and Castaic. It is said
that Piru took its name from its own Shoshonean dialect, *Pi-idhuku*, meaning a sedge or grass.

In only one of these village names do we find the
ending which signified in the Gabrielino dialect "the
place of." We see this ending today, in a Spanish form,
in surviving Indian place names such as Cucamonga
and Cahuenga. Hugo Reid in his list of "lodges" or
"rancherias," prepared in 1852, turned the "n" and the
"g" about. His Cahuenga is *Cahueg-na*. Elsewhere in
his famous "letters" to "The Los Angeles Star" he gives
a short Gabrielino vocabulary, directing that "gn" be
pronounced as in French. This is difficult to transcribe
in English phonetics but we know definitely that "n",
or "ng", was pronounced as in "sing."

That *Kawengna* may somewhat resemble the Indian
pronunciation of the name of the modern boulevard is
indicated by its use by Alexander Taylor on his map
published in 1846, which he entitled, "Map of California Tribes." We find there, clearly printed, the names
of such "tribes" as the *Yangnas* and the *Kawengnas*.
On Kroeber's map, which can be found in his "Handbook of the California Indians," only the root, *Kawe*, is
used, but in a paper on Shoshonean dialects he mentions
these locative endings and says that perhaps "ngna" is
intended. This has been adopted for the purposes of the
present study, in order to suggest the nasal "n" of the
pre-Spanish form.

In the early years of the present century John Peabody Harrington, a genius at forming confidential relationships with Indians, used to repeat to his Gabrielino
informants the names of the birthplaces listed in the
old Baptismal Registers of the San Gabriel and San
Fernando Missions. Some they could not recall and it is
quite possible that in many cases these had been un-
important hamlets of a few families not too well known
in their heydeys.

For the rancherias which these 20th Century survivors could remember they gave Harrington many, and surprising, variants. One can imagine the confusion of the European priests trying to transcribe in their own phonetics the strange names of birthplaces diffidently given by their shy converts, but it is nothing to the tangle presented to our Anglo-American eyes when we attempt to filter the lost Indian pronunciations through that 18th Century Spanish alphabet.

For example, one finds on a list made from the San Fernando Mission Baptismal Register the two names *Cahuenga* and *Cabuepet*. No casual reader would suspect that these are two versions of the same word. Yet, when John P. Harrington mentioned *Cabuepet* to his Gabrielino friends, the name came back on their lips in three forms, *Kawengna*, *Kawengnavit*, and *Kawepet*. The syllable "vit," "bit" or "pet," depending on how the European ear caught the intermediate sound of the Indian tongue, has been said to be the locative ending in the Serrano tongue, but Harrington's research into the Gabrielino and related dialects brings out that this was an ending which indicated the habitat of an individual, much as a New Yorker adds the "er" to his city's name.

Kawengna meant "Place of the Mountain," perhaps one particular mountain, and the other forms signified "I am a native of the Place of the Mountain." Again, *Topangna* stood for "Place where mountains run out into the sea" and *Topangnavit* meant a native of that place. Both forms were given, one about as often as the other, and it is easy to see that the distinction might not be understood by the priest who made the entry. This would explain why *Yangna*, Los Angeles, appears on the San Gabriel Baptismal Register in the less than impressive form of *Yabit*. The later Spanish resident's reference to himself as an "Angeleño" seems a decided improvement from the standpoint of euphony.

In pronouncing the ancient Indian names we have to see them through Spanish eyes, giving the European values to the vowels and automatically saying "h" for the "j," and for the frequently recorded "x" an "h" sounding a little like the German "ch." In most cases

Mission Indian baskets, probably Gabrielino.

we shall have to guess what syllable to accent, though it might be well to follow the Spanish rules for that also.

The old Mission records show that three languages were spoken at San Fernando. Since the encircling mountains mark the borders these languages were undoubtedly Chumash, Serrano and Gabrielino. On the Baptismal Register appear such familiar names as *Secpe* (Sespe) and *Simij* (Simi) of Chumash origin and such definitely Spanish names as Encino and Escorpion, where there were villages of Gabrielinos. There seems to be no record of the Indian name of the rancheria at Encino, which was large and important in its day. El Escorpion, at the extreme west end of San Fernando Valley, was one of the last of the original tracts to be subdivided. Here was located a Gabrielino village known as *Tototngna,* "The Place of the Stones." Tradition said that all the inhabitants of this rancheria died of smallpox.

Although the San Fernando Mission Register lists one birthplace as "Calabzas," no Gabrielino village at that place was recalled by John P. Harrington's informants. What seemed more important to them in the vicinity of the modern Calabasas was a peak in the

Santa Monica Mountains which had been to the Indians a well-known landmark. *Asawtngna,* "Place of the Eagle," they called it, saying that it resembled a great, black eagle with folded wings. This angular formation of dark rock topping symmetrical slopes, west of Seminole Hot Springs, can be viewed from several points in the Santa Monica Mountains. From Highway 101 at the Los Angeles-Ventura county line one looks back to it across the oak-dotted grasslands of El Triunfo Canyon. We might think of it as a lonely sentinel overlooking a portion of the ancient border between the Gabrielinos and their Chumash neighbors. To the Indians it had a far deeper significance, as will be made plain through a study of their religious symbolism.

The Eastern Borderland

A Study of the Cultural Elements

In the Tejon Pass country, through which the highway which is known as the Ridge Route emerges from the mountain barriers between Los Angeles and Bakersfield, there lived in olden times a tribe of Indians who were fierce wizards and sorcerers. At least they were known as such by their fellow Shoshoneans, the Gabrielinos. These men, it was said, could turn themselves at will into bears, and their spirits after death, temporarily at any rate, entered into the bodies of these fearsome animals. As a matter of fact the Gabrielinos believed this of certain of their own shamans, but distance and unfamiliarity tended always to magnify their uneasy respect for anyone who was reputed to possess supernatural powers.

These Tejon Indians, whom we call the *Kitanemuk*, as well as two tribes, the *Alliklik* of the upper Santa Clara River Valley and the *Vanyume* of the Mohave River, the latter now practically if not entirely extinct, Shoshoneans all, are classified under the general head-

ing of Serranos, a Spanish name signifying "mountaineers." This term is more specifically applied, however, to a fourth group, next-door neighbors of the Gabrielinos, who occupied the San Gabriel and San Bernardino Ranges and the canyons on the north side of
San Jacinto Peak, and had a few substantial toeholds
on the fertile lowlands as well.

The Serranos also held the great passes, the Cajon,
which is now like a national Main Street since it carries
Highway 66, and San Gorgonio, through which the
week-end ribbon of traffic flows to Palm Springs and
great produce trucks roar cityward from the ranches
of Coachella and Imperial Valleys. Whether or not
these Indians occupied the plains where now are located
the cities dominated by Redlands, Riverside and San
Bernardino is a question on which differing opinions
are held.

Kroeber's map, Plate 57, accompanying his "Handbook of the Indians of California," shows no Gabrielinos
east of a line running roughly south from Cucamonga
Peak and this line is stoutly defended by those who
have done the most recent archeological work in western San Bernardino county. Here very ancient sites
show no pottery and the points are those of the *atlatl*,
the throwing spear which antedates the bow and arrow.
Later sites, immediately pre-Spanish, contain pottery
that is of a Serrano type. As the Gabrielinos made no
pottery, this would seem to shut them out of the disputed arc of land that now supports the three cities.
Kroeber in his text, however, mentions the possibility
of Gabrielino occupancy of land as far east as Riverside.

Our concern over boundaries might have seemed
amusing to the Indians in question although they them-
serves were acutely aware of small differences in speech.
The Indians of San Gabriel, for example, were said to
have spoken in a "heavier tone" than those of San Fernando, though the dialects were practically identical.
Yet this awareness seemed not to carry over into a definite concept of themselves as belonging to a large, over-
all, organized group of the sort we designate as a "tribe."
The Gabrielinos may have been verging toward such

an idea but with them, as with their mountain-dwelling neighbors, their distinguishing names were those of the village or the clan unit, and their loyalties belonged to their relatives and close associates and to the familiar terrain where they lived and bathed and gathered their food.

Hugo Reid reported that the Gabrielinos had no name for themselves as a tribe. The name "Kizh" or "Kiz," assigned to them a century ago, apparently without much reason, was short-lived. It comes from *kiy*, the word for "house," which is not a typical choice for a tribal name. It is quite common for a group to refer to themselves in their own language simply as "people" or "men," implying a unique value which we have to translate as "The People." In this vein another term, "Tobikhars," translated as "settlers," is better understood as "Tobohar," the mythical first man, but in order to know how this came to be suggested as the tribal name one would have to know how it was obtained. If no clear concept of "the tribe" existed in the informant's mind the questioner may have weighted the reply incorrectly.

On the other hand, all the tribes were quite clear when it came to giving names to others. To the Gabrielinos the Cahuilla were "Easterners," *Kumitaraxam;* and the Santa Barbara Chumash were *Pavajmkar*, from *Pavavit*, "in the water." Paiutes, "two days out on the desert," were dubbed the *Mamajtam*. The Luiseños called the Gabrielinos *Tumangamal-um*, "northerners." Strong recorded the name *Kisianos* as a Cahuilla term for the "Gravelinos," which may have been the source of the term "*Kizh*."

It is natural for modern man, as Kroeber so aptly phrases it, to "hanker after the specific." We have a feeling for dates, eras and boundaries and will go to any length to satisfy it. For that reason future archeological discoveries along this controversial borderline will be watched with interest.

Investigations by ethnologists have tended to give the Gabrielinos much more leeway to the east. The informants of William Duncan Strong, during his intensive work among the Shoshonean groups in 1924-25, told him of three clans of Gabrielinos who had villages in Redlands, Crafton and San Bernardino respectively, all of which, oddly enough, were woven into the reciprocal ceremonial life of the Serrano clans which surrounded them. It is possible that the women in these little settlements learned also to make pottery of the Serrano type, thereby thoroughly confusing the record for the modern archeologist. This surmise does nothing to minimize the Gabrielino preference for cooking pots of Catalina soapstone but merely acknowledges the greater distance to the sea and the corresponding difficulty in procuring such prized items.

Strong concluded that the problem of distribution was largely one of "locating individual groups, not of plotting out tribal domains." The ceremonial reciprocity, which was reported to him in regard to the three villages of Gabrielinos and the surrounding Serranos, he found to exist throughout a wide area. One grouping, he found, "extended as far as San Gabriel to the west, Saboba to the south, and Twenty Nine Palms to the east." In fact, it appeared that a loose ceremonial union existed "between all the Cahuilla, Serrano, Luiseño, and Gabrielino clans who inhabited the territory from San Gorgonio Pass west to the Pacific Ocean."

G. Hazen Shinn, whose informal memoirs were based on personal friendships with Serrano and Cahuilla Indians beginning in 1885, was told by them of the "prehistoric Gabrielino village of Homhoa," which before his time had been occupied by the Serranos, who nevertheless freely acknowledged a prior ownership. *Homhoa* existed at a spot between the present Colton Avenue and the Southern Pacific railroad tracks east of the Santa Ana River, on lands that were taken over by the San Gabriel Mission fathers in 1810, now in Colton.

From 1810 until 1819, when the erection of more substantial buildings was begun, the priests from the Mission came occasionally to read the mass under a brush shelter or "ramada." In the latter year a 12-mile irrigating ditch, or "zanja," was dug from Mill Creek, the Indians using their pointed, wooden digging sticks

and shoulder blades of slaughtered cattle for implements. The restored buildings of what was planned to
be the San Bernardino Assistencia, begun in 1830 but
destined never to be completed, may now be visited by
the public. They are on Barton Avenue just east of the
San Timoteo Canyon Road, near Redlands. Not far
away, on Cottonwood Row, an historical marker notes
the site of the Indian village of *Guachama*. This was
the location of the Mission granary where was stored
the harvest from the wheat fields of the broad Mission
lands which stretched all the way to Yucaipa, a known
Serrano village.

Shinn reported that this *Guachama* was not the original Indian rancheria of that name and this opinion is
supported by archeological data, since no great length
of occupancy was indicated by the findings at this place.
He believed the original site to have been on Bunker
Hill in San Bernardino and the first rude brush "chapel" of the Padres at that spot also, but it would seem
nothing has been learned either to verify or refute this.

Names similar to *Guachama* are associated with several places in this area. Strong's informants mentioned
the Serrano clan, the *Wa-atcem*, whose lands were on
the south slope of the San Bernardino Mountains between the Santa Ana River and Mill Creek, while those
of J. P. Harrington told of a village of *Wa-atngna* in
San Bernardino. Swanton lists a *Wachavak* at the point
where San Timoteo comes out on the Santa Ana River.
Although not a few archeological sites have been found
in the San Bernardino region recent surveys could dis-
cover nothing at this latter point and possibly winter
storms have obliterated it. The Cahuillas who moved
into that location in historic times were decimated by
smallpox.

Shinn worked out an ingenious etymology for the
word *Guachama*, reaching the conclusion that it meant
"plenty to eat." In another region the descendant of an
old Spanish family recalled that *huacho* was the Gabrielino word for "high," and this would possibly tally
with Shinn's own location of the village on a hill. The
Guachpet of the Baptismal Register probably refers to

individuals from this rancheria, which was only one of
many strung out along the bench lands bordering the
Santa Ana River and its larger tributaries.

Although Hugo Reid set the Cucamonga line as the
eastern border of Gabrielino settlement, he wrote in
1852 — 18 years after the secularization decree resulted
in the dissipation of the Mission properties and in what
must have been a general contraction of the Gabrielino
borders. It is a well-known historical fact that certain
Cahuillas were invited into the San Gorgonio Pass and
the San Bernardino Valley to help guard the border
ranches, and that earlier infiltrations had occurred at
the time of the establishment of the Mission agricultural
and stock-raising activities.

The sons of Antonio Maria Lugo, who with Diego
Sepulveda received title to the Rancho San Bernardino
in 1842, found their lands practically untenable, and
many another ranchero woke to find himself a poorer
man after one of the not too infrequent forays by daring bands from the desert. Paiute Indians from as far
away as Nevada, "renegade" Mission Indians, and a
few whites of the more unsavory types among the
"mountain men," joined to sweep down to the valley
ranges, feast on beef, and depart, undeterred and often
unseen, driving before them strings of the most valuable horses they could round up. The rancheros and
other citizens who gathered to trace these bands sometimes failed to catch a glimpse of them, sometimes
found themselves out-numbered and out-fought, and
seldom returned with any of the stolen mounts. On at
least one occasion this failure seemed to be the direct
result of too attractive hospitality offered by the very
haciendados who had suffered the loss.

The example of the daring marauders was too much
for the comparatively peaceful but often hungry Serranos, who learned a similar stealth and daring. San
Dimas Canyon offered them a royal pathway to beef
and fast horses, and once over the ridges along Mount
San Antonio their retreat led down into many a devious
canyon, such as Lytle Creek, through which they could
vanish. A stroll in San Dimas Foothill Park affords the

modern resident a vista of this ancient route, perhaps not too unlike its aspect in Serrano times.

Like the Gabrielinos the mountain Indians have been greatly diminished in number, but proportionately they have had a greater survival. They were a small group from the first and there remain about 100 survivors, eking out a difficult existence on the San Manuel Reservation near Patton, California. Since the greater number of Serranos who have lived on into historic times belonged to the Mariña clan most of the neighboring Indians called the whole band by some form of the root-word *Mara*, or *Moronga.*

It is said that the Gabrielinos looked down on their Serrano neighbors as "country hicks" but they must have accorded grudging admiration to these folk who roamed the mountains and foothills, which were infested with formidable grizzlies. Shinn quotes Daniel Sexton, a well-known citizen and intrepid bear-hunter of a century ago, who witnessed the pathetic awe with which an Indian, coming unexpectedly face to face with a bear on the trail, would stand motionless, imploring the animal to turn aside and spare a life.

The Palm Springs Cahuilla informants of William Duncan Strong told him, "When a man or woman met a California grizzly bear in the mountains he called the latter *piwil* (great-grandfather) and talked soothingly to him thus, 'Beware! Hide yourself far back in the mountains. Your enemies are coming. I am only looking for my food, you are human and understand me, take my word and go away.' The bear would stop, hold up his paws like arms, then dropping to all fours he would scratch dirt to one side. This meant peace and he would go away. 'One must never talk about the bear in the night time, for at night the bear travels, and by day he usually sleeps. If you talk about him at night, earth or rocks or mountains tell him what you say. He listens until he hears where you are going to hunt and goes there, so you will surely be killed'."

In 1843 the Lugos established Michael White, who was known as Miguel Blanco, on land near Camp Cajon, the Rancho Muscupiabe, as an outpost to stem the forays of the Paiute Indians and their cohorts. The venture lasted only a year as the raiders were many and determined and the ranch could not be defended. At this place was the Serrano village, recorded as *"Amutskupiavit,"* described by the Indians who recalled it as located "at the point in the big canyon." Another village in this area derived its title, *Amupke*, from the Serrano word for "nose," because of the shape of a mountain which came to a point. It is possible that these two names refer to the same place or that the general conformation of the surrounding mountains ran to points reminiscent of the human nose. One can perhaps see such a resemblance in the mountain spurs that jut out along the lower reaches of Lytle Creek. A known Serrano site stretches for some distance between the Creek and the present Terrace Road for almost the entire distance between Baseline Street and Highland Avenue in San Bernardino.

"Amutskupiavit," at Camp Cajon, and *Nilengla*, near Arrowhead Springs, were two places where the Gabrielinos said their ancestors had camped, "naked and cold, at the beginning of the world, when the earth was still soft." For every landmark to be seen the Gabrielinos had their own legends or shared those of their neighbors, clothing nature with the bright fabric of their dreams and visions.

Tehovan, near Redlands, and *Sokava*, in the range of hills west of Riverside, were great rocks "who had once been people." At Jurupa, in a cave, lived "a rattlesnake of long ago," but it was without horns. The one with horns lived near the "sharp white hill called *Jungna'a*." The "sharp, white hill" is undoubtedly Slover Mountain, near Colton, which overlooks several very ancient sites. These have yielded no arrowheads but numbers of points of *atlatl* darts, the throwing spears of an earlier period.

The Jurupa Mountains near Riverside were also "sharp and white," and both these and Slover Mountain are now rapidly disappearing, as the cement companies which own them transport for the use of the building industry the calcium carbonate which gives them their startling whiteness. Jurupa was the early name of Riverside, although one early map shows both names. The Gabrielino form was *Hurungna* and a plural word signifying the natives of that place was given as *Huruvitam*, just as the plural of *Yabit*, a resident of Los Angeles, was *Yavitam*. A phrase which occurred to an old Gabrielino when discussing the Jurupa Mountains was "where they went down," perhaps referring to an old trail, but he also gave the meaning of the word *jungna'a* as "buzzard." Considering the tenacity of these birds in clinging to their aeries on the "sharp, white mountains," we can perceive a connection. For many years these birds rose in the air to scold noisily as each blast of dynamite gave them notice of their eventual dispossession.

One of the great legends which was shared by all of these Shoshonean-speaking tribes concerned the supernatural figure known as *Takwis*, for whom Tahquitz Peak, which looms over Palm Springs, was named. *Takwis* was a cannibal whose headquarters was a cave on nearby Lily Peak. He is associated with meteors and with ball lightning, terrifying phenomena. A Gabrielino legend tells of *Tukupar*, the Sky, which was another name for their sacred figure, the raven, going to beard *Takwis* in his lair, outwitting him and recovering the hair which was all that was left of his son, whom the cannibal had devoured. This seems rather a sour victory. Later *Takwis* was killed, but almost immediately revived, and went on to terrify countless generations of Indians who shuddered when thunder, rumbling between the peaks, told of his nocturnal prowlings.

Mount San Jacinto, which the Gabrielinos called *Jamiwu*, was also considered the home of *Takwis*. Other names were *Hidakupa* for the San Gabriel range, *Piwipwi* and *Akvangna* for Bear Mountain and San Gorgonio, respectively. The only word which seemed to be associated with Mount San Antonio, popularly known as Baldy, was the term for "snow," *joat*. These were some of the great upthrusts that ringed the valley lands and gave shape and color to the Shoshonean world.

Most of our knowledge of the social, political and

Gabrielinos building a thatched hut (from a diorama by Elizabeth Mason).

religious systems of these tribes comes from the work of anthropologists and ethnologists among survivors of the Serrano, Luiseño, and Cahuilla clans, and even among those of the very small independent group known as the Cupeño, whose eviction from their ancient stronghold at Warner's Hot Springs came to public notice through the Helen Hunt Jackson novel "Ramona." The largest group of all, the Gabrielino, disappeared before much systematic inquiry had been made. Without the writings of Hugo Reid and Father Geronimo Boscana we should be poor, indeed. The informants of John P. Harrington, early in our own century, added considerably to our knowledge of the cultural elements and their comments on the place-names are sparkling highlights from a vanished era. The research of Kroeber and some others has preserved for us information otherwise lost.

It is from these sources and from the larger body of material gathered from the neighboring tribes that we can obtain as clear a picture as we have of life among the Gabrielinos. We know, for example, that individuals took their clan memberships through the father's side of the family. Since matriarchy was also an ancient pattern and still exists in many Indian tribes, this is an important basic trait. We know also that the Gabrielinos were in contact with bands which maintained two basic divisions or parties, which are called, in scientific parlance, "moieties," and that it is probable the Gabrielinos were similarly organized with moieties which were dubbed "Coyote" and "Wildcat," as they were among the Serranos.

A Gabrielino village might be made up of members of one clan or of several and the chief would be, in all probability, the leader of the dominant clan, or perhaps that of the first settlers. Ordinarily the son of a chief became his successor, although in cases of evident incapability a more able male descendent was chosen, since any new chief needed the approval of the community before he took office. The leader's title was formed from the root name of his village with the addition of the ending "pik" or "vik." Hugo Reid gave this

ending as "ie," and reported that all the chief's immediate relatives bore special titles, the eldest son's being
Tomear and that of the eldest daughter *Manisar*. Re-
gents were chosen in case the male heir was too young
to accede to office, and, in rare instances, a female
descendant was chosen as leader. Ordinarily each rancheria was entirely independent politically but there
were cases, like that of the San Pedro area, where a
considerable number of populous settlements seem to
have been ruled by one chief.

The chief had certain prerogatives like the ownership of the eagles and aeries and custody of certain
sacred regalia and properties. By reason of his office he
was a man of wealth, but he was also required to dis-
pense large quantities of food and property, such as
shell money and other beads, to visiting officials and
guests on public occasions. It was considered a virtue
for him to impoverish himself. For this reason he alone,
among his monogamous clansmen, was allowed to mar-
ry two or more women whose combined efforts were
supposed to replenish his depleted stores of acorns and
seeds to a point beyond that which other families were
able to accumulate. These were also supplemented by
a custom of required "gifts" from his people.

For each clan or village there was also a cult chief
whom the Gabrielinos called the *Paha*. He was an-
nouncer, treasurer and general assistant. Wise old men
became orators who gave moral lectures to the young,
and the *Paha* himself delivered many an educational
discourse sitting atop a wickiup in lieu of a pulpit. We
may be certain that his young auditors found nothing
to smile about in the speaker's words or his appearance.
Respect bordering on awe was accorded the elders, especially those of high degree.

Another official was the *Takwa*, the "Divider of
Food," whose duties probably included the manage-
ment of the elaborate ceremonies of mourning for the
dead. A subtle thread of association connects this title
with the name of *Takwis*, the supernatural figure with
the cannibalistic tendencies. For the boy's initiation
rites there was probably a separate official, as well as a

special fire-tender for the mourning observances. Rabbit drives and other activities of an economic nature were headed by capable persons and Reid was told of apt and swift-footed boys being educated as messengers and serving in that capacity as long as their memories and legs would serve them.

We know very little of Gabrielino warfare, but it is probable that the chief or a war leader appointed by him led such expeditions, and we know that a council of war was called together by an official crier who also gave the signal for the actual mobilization and onset of the action. Father Boscana paints an interesting picture of the war procession, the young men close behind the leader, followed by the old men, while the women and children brought up the rear, carrying seedmeal mush that had been in preparation for days. Contributions of meal had been exacted of the prospective warriors' wives so that no one would go hungry. During the action, which was supposed to surprise the enemy but seldom did, the women gathered up the arrows that had been discharged in their direction and delivered them to their own fighters to be used as ammunition.

These engagements were not fought for conquest but entirely as matters of revenge, sometimes for affronts suffered generations earlier and left unavenged, perhaps because the means to a decisive victory appeared insufficient. The councils appear to have been concerned with this one very practical issue. If success could be achieved with additional forces, and a friendly clan could be induced to furnish them, the chief of the second clan was sent a present of the greatest value possible to spare. Reasons for feeling affronted were the failure of a chief to return the customary gift at a ceremonial, thefts of anything of even slight value, the abduction of a woman, or the knowledge that witchcraft had been practiced in an adverse way.

The fights were not prolonged but they were deadly. If the adversaries could not retrieve their wounded they were sure to be despatched on the field. Men prisoners were decapitated and women and children became slaves. Trophies could be redeemed by payments but the luckless slaves could achieve freedom only by escape or recapture. Fr. Boscana believed these trophies to be scalps of the male prisoners, but it is quite possible that the hair, representing the spirit of the victim, was taken, not the scalp.

Hugo Reid wrote a very humorous paragraph describing the custom of verbal wars which begs to be quoted in full. "Animosity between persons or families was of long duration, particularly between those of different tribes," he wrote. "These feuds descended from father to son until it was impossible to tell how many generations. They were, however, harmless in themselves, being merely a war of songs, composed and sung against the conflicting party, and they were all of the most obscene and indecent language imaginable.—There are two families at this day whose bad feelings commenced before Spaniards were even dreamt of and they still continue yearly singing and dancing against each other. The one resides at the Mission of San Gabriel, and the other at San Juan Capistrano: they both lived at San Bernardino when the quarrel commenced. During the singing they keep stamping on the ground to express the pleasure they would derive from tramping on the grave of their foes. Eight days was the duration of the song fight."

Among the Serranos ceremonial activity was assigned in such a way that one clan furnished the cult chief and the "dance house" or ceremonial enclosure, while an associated clan contributed the ceremonial assistant and the sacred bundle of fetish material that constituted the altar or focal point of worship. Since two such groups, to quote Strong, "commonly intermarried, and were of the opposite moieties, their reciprocal relationship is obvious."

We do not know whether or not the Gabrielinos pressed this division of social and religious activities to such a fine point, although Strong was told that the three groups remembered to have lived in San Bernardino, Crafton, and Redlands were thus interwoven with the nearby Serrano clans. It is reported by observers of Indian ceremonies of all these tribes that apparently

Toloache mortar (see Page 57).

casual visitors from other villages received gifts of food and shells, and at the conclusion of weddings certain onlookers divested the bride of her finery, which consisted of shell beads, feathers and flowers. Actually these things were fees, legally due to those who had been officially invited to make the necessary arrangements.

Clan members were not permitted to intermarry and close relatives on the mother's side probably also were barred from mating. A spontaneous attraction between a young couple could lead to a formal agreement and payment to the bride's family. Sometimes very small children were betrothed by the parents. The ceremony of marriage consisted of a procession, leading or even carrying the girl to the hut where her bride-groom sat alone awaiting her. At this point the guests, among them the officials from another clan who had arranged the affair, departed to continue the festivities with singing, dancing and feasting. The husband had spent a period preceding the ceremony in the wife's mother's home, observing the bride-to-be in the role of his prospective seed-gatherer and technician of mortar and pestle, but the final place of residence was in the village of the husband's father. After this move the wife was not supposed to visit her relatives but they were free to come to her home.

Barrenness and incompatibility were grounds for divorce, the husband's family being reimbursed for the marriage payment. The woman's relatives began immediately to plan a new marriage for her. Deliberate incest was punishable by death and infidelity in wed-lock theoretically so, but the latter usually resulted in a simple exchange of spouses, since the wronged husband had a legal right to take the wife of the evildoer, and this solution meant less effort to all concerned. Undoubtedly some promiscuity occurred, especially during prolonged religious dances, but little stigma seemed attached to this. Venereal disease did not exist among them and all children were considered legitimate.

Few if any infectious diseases dogged these people until the advent of the Spanish when the consequent lack of immunity played an immense part in the weaving of their doom. As young boys and girls were deliberately excluded from the immediate circle around the fire and all but the women went entirely naked it may be possible that weaklings died out early, leaving a race which we know was genetically stable, physically hardy, and attuned to the conditions of its environment.

In appearance these people were not tall, but stocky, muscular, and well-fleshed. Their skin was not as dark as that of certain other California tribes, but a soft, warm brown, even rather fair in childhood. A report to this effect made by the Cabrillo expedition of Catalina Islanders gave rise to some fantastic notions of a special race of "white Indians" being found there at that time. The women postponed the browning and wrinkling effect of the weather as long as possible with the liberal use of red ochre paint, but the girls used this more tastefully, as rouge, with an eye to vanity. Both men and women fancied tattooing on the forehead, the women sometimes preferring a decoration of the chin and sometimes an area from the eyes down to the breast. The skin was pricked with a thorn or a tiny fragment of flint, whereupon charcoal from the yucca cabbage, called in Spanish "mescal," or the juice of nightshade leaves, was rubbed into the small, bleeding wounds, making a strong blue-black tattoo. The young girls were tattooed before puberty.

Stone mortar and pestle.

All of the early European observers of these Indians were struck with the deliberate and unabashed nudity of the men and children. The women, quite modest in contrast, wore aprons made of narrow, flexible strips of the inner bark of cottonwood or willow, hung in back, and frontflaps of many strands of twine formed from the fibers of dogbane or milkweed. Sometimes the apron at the back was of deerskin, and the men occasionally sported a small deerskin cape for the shoulders. A robe made of twisted strips of rabbit fur, woven together with milkweed or yucca-fiber twine, was useful at night, as were deerskins. On the islands and along the coast robes made of otterskin were to be seen. Farther inland they would have been a princely possession. As a rule everyone went barefoot, although yucca-fiber sandals were used in rough country.

A daily bath was an inflexible rule for old and young, so that, as the Luiseños told their children, "the moon will see you clean." The family dried about the fire as breakfast was being prepared and that, too, preferably was finished before the sun was fully up. Besides this daily incidental wetting the hair was kept glossy by occasional applications of clay, which was left to dry and then broken away in hard cakes from the thick, black tresses, undoubtedly removing thereby any parasites which might have found a lodging there.

The men wore their hair long, usually parted in the middle and falling straight or braided at the back, doubled upward and secured with a cane or bone hairpin. They also fancied a horse-tail coiffure. The women liked bangs and long, free tresses over their shoulders. They shortened their hair in mourning, widows in particular cropping theirs close to the scalp. This was a real sacrifice and a mark of their intense feeling of loss, since the hair was symbolic of the spirit, and also touched feminine vanity in a weak spot. The shortening was accomplished by singeing. What little hair grew on the men's faces was removed by plucking. A cord of human hair was used to secure the pad or wig to which the men secured the feathers that made up the ceremonial headdress.

Flowers were used liberally for adornment, as boas, in the hair or over the ear. And no girl was without her beads of shell, some of them unbelievably tiny, an eighth of an inch and even less in diameter. Larger beads were formed of dark steatite, whalebone, or of whole olivella shells, while those of thick, half-inch clam shell doubled as ornaments or money. These clam shell beads had a definite value as a medium of exchange, the unit being measured by a string of them circling the fist. Earrings of cane were worn by the men while the women fancied shell rings hung with cylindrical pendants of whale's tooth, festooned with feathers. The men may have worn a cane tube through the pierced nasal septum, although Reid was told they did not do so.

Most of the simple belongings of these people were of a perishable nature, with the notable exception of the utensils used in the preparation of food. The Gabrielinos used mortars in the bedrock, as did most of the Indians in the later periods in California, but they also made round portable mortars which in some areas of the state were relics of earlier inhabitants and regarded by the late comers as being of supernatural origin. Metates—flat, portable slabs for grinding—had dropped from general use in these later times but some of the people still used them, sinking them slightly in the ground and turning them over from time to time. Probably they also knew the use of the basket-hopper, a bottomless basket asphalted to a mortar or even a flat pounding stone, which was a device found among neighboring tribes.

These utensils offer a field of comparative study to the archeologist, since the metate and mano appear to be most useful in the grinding of hard-kerneled seeds and the mortar and pestle are ideally suited to the reduction into meal of the softer acorn. Certainly the brave pioneers who first experimented with the distinctly bitter acorn, devising ways of leaching out the tannin and making it edible, opened the way for the settlement of the oak country of Southern California to the migrating peoples as surely as gasoline refining techniques contributed to the more recent swelling of the population. A continuation of present research tending to establish an evolution of techniques of food preparation may help toward clearing up California's obscure prehistory. A comparison of the very crude stone choppers found in the most ancient sites with the exquisitely turned Gabrielino pestle, to which they gave the name 'aman, "it's hand," causes even an amateur to ponder on these things.

Undoubtedly the Gabrielino women knew something of the art of pottery but did not practice it where they could procure the steatite, or soapstone, pots from Santa Catalina Island. These were superior articles. One could hardly induce food to burn in one of them; they could be mended with asphalt if broken, or a handle be affixed to turn a large fragment into a frying pan. Steatite also appeared among their belongings in the shape of pipes, beads, fine ceremonial bowls and carvings of whales, seals, fish and other animals, and even baby powder made by scraping the soft stone into fine dust.

The strong fibers of the yucca root made excellent brushes for the hair or to clean old meal from utensils. Sticks were formed into loops for lifting hot stones in toasting or boiling in baskets; gourds were used for dippers. Platters and bowls were carved from wood. An abalone shell could be turned into a shallow bowl by plugging its apertures with asphalt, sometimes with the inset of a shell bead as an expression of the artistic impulse.

Hugo Reid wrote that the Gabrielino baskets were so well known as to require no description, little thinking that the next century would relegate both the baskets and the makers, to all practical purposes, into a class with the fabled Dodo. We have, however, a few examples, and many more of the work of other "Mission Indians," so that we can form a good idea of the splendid artistry which had been achieved in this field. Both coiled and twined baskets were made, and for a multitude of purposes. The acorn harvest was brought to the village in cone-shaped carrying baskets hung on the backs of the sturdy women, to be stored in huge basket-like granaries on platforms. Foreheads were protected from the carrying-net by round basket-caps. There were seed-beaters, winnowing baskets, and parching baskets. Boiling baskets into which heated rocks were successively introduced until the mush was cooked, though still used by people farther north, had been superseded by steatite cooking pots. Water bottles with necks and flat bottoms were coated with asphalt to reinforce the tightness which was already woven in by the fingers of the skilled artisan. Beyond all these were the ceremonial baskets replete with designs of great beauty.

These Indians grew no corn, not because of stupidity as has been charged, but because the long dry summers precluded its successful introduction. A crop of literally tons of acorns, pounded to meal in mortars and subjected to leachings in leaf-lined sieve baskets set into sand basins, made a satisfactory substitute, especially as the bark of a certain native plant, the *cascara sa-*

grada, could sometimes be chewed to offset a slightly astringent effect. The seeds of various grasses, parched in a basket by hot coals, were fancied, as well as those of a bush which resembled a sage, the *Salvia columbariae*, which the Spanish were to call "chia."

The pits of the wild plum bushes yielded a good seed for grinding into meal. In fact the native fruits were more useful in this fashion than for their pulp, which was often rather sour and dry, but the Indians knew which to choose for cooling drinks and where to find a vegetable chewing gum. The yucca furnished tender shoots to eat, as did certain wild sages. The climate did not encourage berries, though in the marshy thickets a kind of blackberry grew, and on the hills among the chaparral a dry and bitter currant and a thorny gooseberry. Cactus fruit gathered with tongs yielded a quota of food, as did the "honey dew" left by the aphids as a sticky secretion on the plants they fed upon.

Every small and large animal that roamed the plains and foothills, probably even the bear although that is missing from some lists, was hunted or snared to add to the Gabrielino diet. Deadfalls with acorn triggers yielded small game, communal drives sent scores of rabbits into waiting nets, rats' nests were burned and gophers lured from their holes. Hunters went out for deer and antelope equipped with head and back disguises of the animals' antlers and skins and a knowledge of every mannerism of the quarry to make possible the close approach necessary for a clean arrow shot. The range of fish and bird and insect ran from the stranded whale downward to the yellowjacket larva and the caterpillar, which was served after toasting to a crisp.

Hunting was the man's vocation and when it came to large game must have been an undertaking calling for resolute planning and action. The practice of stinging the body, particularly the eyelids, with nettles before going out on a major hunt served as a sort of ritual reminder to the man that he really possessed the power and courage to carry out the expedition with success. A man refrained from sexual relations before and during a hunt and did not eat while engaged in it. There was a taboo against the eating by a hunter of any meat from an animal which he himself bagged. At least in historic times these provisions could be infringed on the sly and a simple exchange on the part of two hunters could ward off real hunger, but the practice would appear to have ensured the bringing home of a considerable share of the meat for the stay-at-homes, and the fair division of it was an official matter. Strong was told of an all-night celebration of a successful hunt by the Serranos consisting of singing and dancing and ceremonial smoking, followed in the morning by the cutting up and distributing of the meat by the *Takwa*, the "Eater," who was also the "Divider of Food."

These men made self-bows about four and one-half feet in length, with two- or three-ply strings of sinew or vegetable fiber. The arrows were usually of cane with a hardwood foreshaft, sometimes with no other head and sometimes with a stone or bone head. The arrows had three radial feathers and sometimes the points were poisoned with rattlesnake venom or boiled-down animal gall. They were carried in a skin quiver on the back, the arrows being pulled out over the shoulder. Bones were sharpened into awls, shoulder blades were used for hide-scrapers, and flakes from cobble stones for cutting tools. Excellent knives of flint were asphalted to wooden handles which were sometimes wrapped in buckskin. Very small and delicate instruments for drilling were fashioned from bits of flint, hafted or held in the fingers with buckskin.

Contrary to the practice of most tribes the dressing of skins was a skill acquired by the men. The hides were cured with brains and wood ashes and softened with rubbing stones over a blunted, inclined rubbing post. Cradles, shaped like a "Y" in the San Fernando area, and like a "U" ladder among the San Gabriel villages, were made by the men, of wood with a hood of skin. The women carried them by means of a strap across the breast or forehead. But they sometimes dispensed with the cradle entirely, putting the baby in the carrying net, as in a hammock, on the back.

String and cordage of all sorts were formed by rolling strands of fiber on the thigh. Both sexes joined in this occupation, which was probably a never-ended task for spare time. Yucca, Indian hemp (*Apocynum*), milkweed (*Asclepius*), nettle (*Urtica*) were the ordinary fibers used, although human hair was used for ceremonial purposes. The strings were rolled in two and four ply, possibly three as well, and rope was formed of several strands of two-ply string.

The huts, which we usually call wickiups from an old word for dwelling learned from the Sac, Fox and Kickapoo tribes, were described by the Spanish as being shaped like half an orange, although some references have been discovered to suggest an occasional pointed shape. The circular framework was of willow and was thatched with tule, carrizo, or grass, leaving an entrance and a smoke hole. The central fireplace gradually lowered as ashes were removed. Very few instances of an additional cover of earth for Gabrielino houses are recorded except for the small structures which were designed for sweat baths, for which the Spanish used the Aztec term "temescal."

As S. F. Cook points out, there can be no doubt that these Indians were capable of prolonged, directed effort whenever such effort was necessary to meet the demands of their way of life. Harvesting of the seeds and acorns could not be postponed; all sorts of tools and utensils and weapons had to be produced from materials which had to be secured by personal effort or by trading for them. Yet none of these happy folk worked one moment beyond the point when the actual needs of the day or the imperative duties of the season had been fulfilled. Sun-bathing was a recognized and respectable occupation and basking in warm springs a luxury for which every Indian yearned.

The western portions of San Bernardino and Riverside counties abound with springs, many of them warm, and this borderland of the Gabrielinos may have been then, as now, resort country to which the prehistoric tourist turned for refreshment. Here society became considerably more cosmopolitan than was normally the case. *Paxauxa* or *Pakhavka*, a village of which the site has been confirmed by archeological data, stood on Temescal Creek in the present Corona. Luiseños and Gabrielinos lived there side by side, and the Santa Ana Mountains were laced with trails by which the coastal Indians reached the coveted warmth of the springs and the desert tribesmen the salt air of the sea.

Paxauxa may be the rancheria which appears in the San Juan Capistrano Baptismal Register as *Axaxa,* since its meaning is to be found in the Gabrielino *Axawkngna,* "in the net." Lake Elsinore, farther south, is in Luiseño territory but the Gabrielinos knew many a place-name there. *Guibanga,* as listed in the San Gabriel Register, was known to them as *We-evungna,* "like the grasshoppers we are here," a name which was also applied to a nearby mountain range and which seems related to that of a Desert Cahuilla clan, *wiitem,* "grasshoppers."

Strong was told that the "old language" of Saboba Hot Springs had been "nearly like Serrano," but for long years the Indian settlement there has been Luiseño. Nearby was *Kujungna,* from the Gabrielino for the word "head," and listed in the San Gabriel Register as *Coyubit.* In the canyon above *Sovovo* lay *Korovangna,* the Register's *Coronababit.* A similar name for a village near Santa Monica meant "we are in the sun."

High above Corona, in the Santa Ana Mountains, lay a small, lush valley with a pool and a "cienega," or marsh, and a view out to the Channel Islands. The village here gave its name to converts of the San Gabriel Mission, the Register reading *Pamaibit,* though the valley was known as *Pamajam,* from the word *pa'ajvar,* "above." Recent archeological excavations make it possible to be sure of its location, hitherto known only through one verbal tradition.

The Southern Borderland

A Study of the Religion

$\mathbf{G}$eographically the boundary between the Gabriel-inos and their southern neighbors is clearly marked at Aliso Creek which empties into the ocean just south of Laguna Beach, and the dialects show marked differences. Yet when we embark upon a study of the religious beliefs and practices of the more dominant northern group we find our main source of information among the people we know as Juaneños; and from the survivors among the Luiseños of the San Luis Rey district, even farther south, where an ever-dwindling number of initiates still retain a remnant of the vast body of ceremonial songs and observances which once were the main concern of the influential men of the tribe.

Father Geronimo Boscana wrote his famous "Historical Account of the San Juan Capistrano Indians of Southern California" from observations made during his stay at that Mission from 1812 to 1826. He seems to have furnished the greater part of the information used to answer the 36-part questionnaire issued to the Missions by the Spanish government in 1814, and the request for this information may have aroused his interest. Or it may have been that by temperament he was a born anthropologist. In 1826 he was assigned to the San Gabriel Mission, where he died in 1831 at the age of 55. Apparently he left no material gathered during his stay in San Gabriel, but his signature as an officiating priest in the Church at Los Angeles attests to the many journeys he made in those later years between the Mission and the Pueblo.

Even today the Luiseños attribute the origin of their religious mythology to people of the north, sometimes saying it came to them by way of Santa Catalina and San Clemente. Constance Goddard Du Bois was told, "On the other side of the Mission of San Juan Capistrano there was a large Indian village, and from there the Chungichnish worship was brought to San Luis Rey. San Luis Rey taught Pala, Pala taught Pauma, Pauma taught Potrero, Potrero gave it to La Jolla with the songs and the present manner of dancing." This La Jolla was not on the coast but in the mountains, and from there the chain of proselyting for the Gabrielino religion continued to Warner's Hot Springs, to Mesa Grande and Santa Ysabel. As the last two bands were Diegueños, of the Yuman branch of the Hokan-speaking people, one can see that the strong impetus of this movement penetrated the language barrier. Elements of this religion are thought to have spread northward into Chumash and Yokuts country as well, and it is certain that all these tribes influenced each other in many ways, reciprocally.

By Father Boscana's time the spread of this dominant religion was well under way and it is quite certain that it was accelerated during Mission times. Some Gabrielino birthplaces are listed in the San Juan Capistrano Baptismal Register and a considerable mixing of groups occurred within the Mission settlements. Some of the Padre's informants may have been Gabrielinos and modern researchers agree that the basic myths he recorded had their origin among that group, receiving a special impetus, if not the initial one, from the religious genius of the Gabrielinos whose homes were on the offshore islands.

In a typical migration legend the people of San Juan Capistrano assigned their own origin to a village in Gabrielino country. The name of this place had been *Sehat* or *Suva*, the root word referring to the "wild, burrowing bee," which made its home in the soft mud of a nearby river bank. Patient research on the part of John P. Harrington narrowed the possible location of this village to one of five sites in the region of Los Nietos. The migrants settled in their new country under the leadership of a daughter of the chief of *Suva*.

Of all the rancherias mentioned by Father Boscana the most important is the Gabrielino *Puvu* or *Puvungna*. This was the village "on the other side of San Juan Capistrano" from which the dominant religion spread southward. It stood two miles inland from Alamitos Bay, on land which in our time is known as the Bixby Ranch. The ancient name evoked but one associated phrase from Harrington's informant, "en la vola." It is possible that he meant, in his Shoshonean Spanish, "en la bola." This could carry the connotation, "in the crowd." If so, one might dip back into Father Boscana's story of the migration for a possible clue as to what went on in the old man's mind to bring up such an odd phrase.

It seems that after the people came down from *Suva* they divided for economic reasons into smaller groups, but at a later time were invited by Coronne, their woman chief, to return for a feast at her central village, *Putuidem*. This rancheria existed at one of three possible sites on the lower reaches of Aliso Creek. Coronne, an enormously fat woman, seems to have eaten too heartily of her own repast, dying thereafter and leaving her people to mourn and to ascribe a human origin to one more landmark—a mound that recalled her rotund shape.

On the way home from this great congregation some of the tribesmen stopped at a place near the present San Juan Capistrano, where, in grief, cold and weary, they slept piled up for warmth and comfort. Next day they named the place *Acagchemen*, the meaning of which is given as "a pyramidal form of anything which moves, such as an ant hill." A modern Juaneño transcribes this as *A-hash-amen*, and from this word, it is said, the Juaneños took their tribal name. However, the village of that name is sometimes given as "The Place of the Wild Pea."

At Puvungna also, according to Gabrielino mythology, a great gathering was once held. So many came to a council that they were forced to sleep outside the village limits. Perhaps here also some of the tired and weary visitors from far places slept "en la vola," in a ball, or crowd. The ancient name must have recalled some such memory to have elicited this phrase.

At the great village of Puvungna, at Alamitos, was centered the main weight of the Creation Myth of the coastal Shoshoneans. Limited space permits but a brief outline of a few of the many variations of its main theme, but no understanding of the originators of this significant myth could be reached without some knowledge of its content.

Father Boscana called attention to resemblances between this legend and the account of creation given in Genesis, such as the successive formation of the elements. There are even more striking parallels to be found between this myth and that of the Greek creation story as told in Hesiod, and it is interesting to note that the archaic Greeks were called, with not a little scorn, "acorn-eaters," and considered by the gods to have been pre-human.

The Indians looked back on their own mythological forerunners as not having been people in the strict sense of the word. "They were a species of animal but distinct from those of the present day," wrote Father Boscana. At first there was "nothing, only one above and another below: these two were brother and sister, man and woman, the one above, a man, which is properly the Heaven, and the one below, a woman, which is the Earth, but it was not the Heaven and Earth as they are seen now, but of another nature which they do not know how to explain, and it was continually very dark night, without sun, moon, or stars."

In another version this "Heaven" is definitely named *Nocuma* or *Tukma*, "the night," but the man acts as the bringer of light, "which is the sun." Earth, having given up her initial resistance, six births ensued, earth and sand, rocks of all sorts (especially flints for arrow points), trees and shrubs, medicinal herbs and grasses, wild animals, and, at the last, *Ouiot* or *Wiyot*, who was "an animate being, but different from the rational kind, and irrational." Father Boscana pointed out that in actual life these Indians had taboos against the marriage of close relatives as strict as the Mosaic law. But he did not draw the parallels to be found here with a great number of creation myths from which such ancient customs as the royal marriages of Egypt, considered to be between divinities, drew their sanction.

Wiyot ruled the people for a long time, ever more severely, until at last his sons wished to depose the aging leader. They chose to poison him and were successful, as Coyote kicked over the shell in which *Wiyot's* mother had prepared an antidote. Though Coyote was sent away by a ruse to prevent him from devouring the dead hero's body, he returned in time to leap upon the flaming funeral pyre and to seize and eat a portion of the shoulder.

In a slightly different version Coyote was said to have escaped with the heart "of his father," at a place "where the ground is like the red paint the Indians use for painting their faces." The Luiseños tell of *Wiyot* being taken from hot spring to hot spring but at last dying near Lake Elsinore. In the version quoted above, which contains a rare instance of the name of *Wiyot* from a Gabrielino source, he is said to have died at Big Bear Lake and the only name the Indians had for the lake was "where *Wiyot* died." "At that time," this old informant continued, "white and blue beads came up out of the water and the lake cried like a person. There was no sun or stars, all was dark. All the pines on top of the mountains used to be people who turned to trees when *Wiyot* died. The Indians used to go to the lake and sing and weep there and throw beads into the water."

In Shoshonean mythology nothing is as clear and simple as this outline might seem to indicate. *Wiyot* was in some way associated with the moon, the reappearance of which was regularly greeted with dancing by the old men and a race by the younger ones. Father Boscana recorded a song of the old men, "As the moon dieth and cometh to light again so we, also having to die, will live again." The Luiseños felt that death had not been known before the death of *Wiyot* and that it was then the first people had become changed into stars, rocks and other things which continued to exist.

Wiyot may also have been that legendary "captain" who had led the people southward in the long migration "at the beginning of the world." The Luiseño legend emphasizes that this chieftain had been of humble birth but became Captain-General and assigned to each tribe its own territory. He was said to have gone to dwell in an island paradise in the ocean west of Santa Catalina Island. "God made both worlds," said an old Gabrielino. "The one there is connected and balanced with the one here."

It was after *Wiyot's* death that the great council convened at *Puvungna*, in order to discuss what the people could use for food. Up to that time they had been eating a kind of white clay similar to that used for body paint. Now, as they enumerated the wild food, such as acorns, amaranth and "chia" seeds, and the small and large animals available, a new leader appeared to them, at first seeming like a phantom or an evanescent vision. The people instantly inferred that *Wiyot* had returned, according to his promise so to do. But this being announced himself as a greater chief and, indeed, soon eclipsed the old leader.

The name of this god, *Chinigchinich*, as recorded by Boscana and his first translator, Alfred Robinson, contains one syllable more than the Indians actually used in pronouncing it. Another form used by Kroeber and Du Bois and the later commentators is *Chungichnish*. J. P. Harrington worked it out phonetically with the

Shoshonean nasal "n" as *"Chee-ngich-ngich."* Since the name gradually faded from use by the originators during Mission times there seems to be but one record of anything similar from Gabrielino sources—the one in J. P. Harrington's notes in which "un sabio," a wise man, is translated as *tsinitsnits,* all the "n's" being marked as nasal. A plural, "sabios," is given as *tsinitsitsam.*

A second version, given by Fr. Boscana and attributed to the Juaneños who lived near the coast, begins with *Nocuma,* or "Night," as the creator of the elements and animals. The sea became overcrowded, so Night fastened the earth by means of a large black rock, called the *tosaut,* which was brought to him by a whale. The center of the rock was full of gall which overflowed, causing the sea to become salty and as large as it is now. In this myth first man, as created by the Night, was the ancestor of *Wiyot,* but in both versions *Wiyot* dies and is succeeded by *Chungichnish.*

A good many different names or titles are applied to *Chungichnish,* this most dominant figure in Shoshonean legendry, one being *Attajen,* meaning "man," or "rational being." In some versions he is without parentage, appearing as a spirit to announce his supremacy. In another he is the obscure son of Tacu, which is the Comet, and Auzar. His given name was *Ouiamot* or *Wiyamut.* At the time he assumed leadership he called himself *Chungichnish* and said he came from above. Having listened to the council as it weighed the food problem of the people he gave a great speech in which he set the future course of tribal law and religion.

Chungichnish delegated powers and responsibilities to certain persons, to one rain making, to another the production of clear weather, and so on. Thus began a hierarchy of seers without whose magical intervention and knowledge of the correct songs rain would not fall, seeds would not form, rabbits and ducks would not multiply. The god also created out of mud from the shores of a nearby lake a number of men and women of a new race, people distinct from the descendants of *Wiyot.* He commanded obedience to himself and to all his precepts. Penalties for transgressions were fixed in the forms of being bitten by rattlesnakes, or bears, or other calamities of the sort.

Father Boscana perceived an enigma in this myth and chose to "adhere" to the most reasonable of the explanations given as to what became of the descendants of *Wiyot*. According to this theory they were transformed into people similar to those newly created from the mud of the lake shore. This seemed logical as it preserved the lines of inheritance by which the powers already delegated by *Chungichnish* were to descend throughout the coming generations.

Constance Goddard Du Bois points out that the *Chungichnish* religion was based on fear. An all-seeing eye of an all-powerful god marks a distinct step in the religious perception of a people, and the precepts and taboos which the chiefs and *pahas* expounded to the people constituted not 10 commandments but a myriad of "thou shalt nots," the transgression of any one of which could bring dire consequences. Since *Chungichnish* was associated with the sun it is no wonder the people rose to bathe and breakfast before his vigilant eye took the place of the gentler rule of an earlier, less sternly focused supernatural being, the ever-mourned *Wiyot*, whose name was sometimes given as *Moar*, the Moon.

Chungichnish had three other names besides those already mentioned: *Soar*, *Tobet*, and *Quoar*. (The spelling of the last is taken from a translation by John P. Harrington of a second manuscript of Father Boscana's work). These three names show a progression. *Saor* related to a time "before he knew how to dance," which indicates that the god went through a pre-initiatory period when he was a common man. *Tobet* was his name when he danced in the regalia of feather-fringed skirt and head-tuft, which was itself called the *tobet* and which was worn by all subsequent fully-initiated men while performing the ceremonials which *Chungichnish* taught. The god himself wore this costume when he at last danced away into heaven.

The name *Tobet* seems to be derived from *Toovit*,

Head-tuft of hawk or owl feathers given to tribal initiates.

California Brush Rabbit, who sang at *Wiyot's* funeral, thereby becoming "the first man that ever sang." He was the originator of the mourning ceremonies and all subsequent officials in charge of these observances were called by this name. As *Chungichnish*, in his phase of "The Initiate," was called *Tobet* it may be that he had concluded an obscure period of preparation and was ready at the time of the council at his birthplace, *Puvungna*, to announce himself as prophet and revealer.

With the name *Quoar* the roster of these titles is concluded. Hugo Reid, writing 81 years after the founding of San Gabriel Mission, when the Gabrielinos had already lost much of their facility in their own language, recorded only one of these names, but it is significantly similar to that of the third, or divine, phase of *Chungnichnish*. *Qua-o-ar*, Reid wrote, was the name of the god and creator of the Gabrielinos, a name so sacred it was rarely spoken and then in a hushed tone. Substituted for it in ordinary speech was the term *Y-yo-hariv-guina*, Giver of Life.

Reid was told that the earth was fixed on the shoulders of seven giants and that earthquakes were caused by one of them changing position. The Giver of Life had created man and woman from the earth, assigning to them the names *Tobohar* and *Pabavit*. Many years later an old Gabrielino, when told of Reid's statements, responded with a vague memory that "the woman was in the water still and the man was on dry land." This went back, J. P. Harrington felt, to an obscure legend of a mythical race which had lived in springs and in the country below springs, of which an individual was called *Paavavut*, or water-woman, a parallel to our own and the Serrano Indians' "Water Babies."

Tobohar, the name of the first man, recalls the term for the "whole world," *Tobangnar* or *Tovangnar*, which

Eagle feather kilt worn by dancers.

— 46 —

Reid transcribed as Yobangnar. This was also the name of the sacred ceremonial enclosure. Reid described this as having been 50 feet in diameter and formed of stakes set in the ground to a height of three feet and entwined basket-fashion with willow twigs. Only "the old men who knew" could enter it, although Reid said that the chiefs, seers and initiates were sometimes joined by boys in training and women singers, and, during memorial services, by the close relatives of those who were mourned.

Father Boscana gave a detailed description of this "temple" as he saw it at San Juan Capistrano, where it was called *Vanquech* or *Wamkich*. There the enclosure seems to have been smaller in diameter but high enough to preclude seeing into it from the outside. It was formed of mats of tules and contained an inner enclosure in which was placed a bundle of feathers, claws, beaks and horns of those birds and animals which were sacred to *Chungichnish*, acting as his observers and agents of retribution. This bundle was enclosed in a coyote skin. A Cahuilla version of it was wrapped in a mat supposed to be woven of rushes found only near the sea, but in later years it was made of a sharp-pointed grass found in the mountains of their own region.

Uninitiated men and women were not allowed to enter the *Wamkich* which Father Boscana observed, and the young people did not dare to approach it. The enclosure was dedicated anew for each ceremony and, to make sure that no inexpert or irreverent act would occur within the sacred walls, rehearsals were held in a similar structure which had not been dedicated.

Among the numerous rites scheduled during a year those held in honor of the recent dead were of great importance. Of some related groups enough is known so that the exact order and names of the memorial observances can be given; but we can only surmise of the Gabrielinos, since they were the originators of the basic religion, that they also had a comprehensive cycle of songs accompanied by dancing, and a protocol in regard to exchanges of gifts and fees and to the prerogatives of the officials from visiting clans which would have done credit to the present Department of State.

In later prehistoric times many Gabrielino villages had adopted cremation in preference to direct burial. It was the custom to throw some of the property of the deceased onto the flaming funeral pyre, retaining the greater part to be destroyed during the extended community observance which ordinarily was celebrated once a year. Certain Cahuilla bands planned to hold this when the constellation Orion, which they called *pa'tem*, Mountain Sheep, was overhead. For the Gabrielinos we know only that autumn was the usual time, after the harvest of seeds and acorns. Undoubtedly their celebrations included many or all of the specific acts reported from neighboring groups, with a climax in the spectacular "burning of the images," figures made to represent each of the persons who had died since the last great mourning ceremony had been performed.

Reid mentioned eight days of preparation and training for inexperienced participants and an equal period for the actual celebration, the first day of which was spent in dedicating the ceremonial enclosure, after which the "feast" began. As he phrased it, "The singers (women) were seated in a circle around the church, leaving only the doorway free. The men and children, adorned with eagle and hawk feathers and a plentiful supply of paint laid on the face, neck, arms and upper part of the body, proceeded to dance, being governed in the operation by numerous gestures, both of hands and feet, made by the seers. Each dancer represented some animal in his movements; but the growl given simultaneously at the end of each verse, was for the bear."

During the dances poles stood at the four points of the compass within the *Wamkich*. Each was about 10 feet high, with a braid of weaving hanging from the top into both sides of which were inserted feathers from the sacred eagles. The walls of the enclosure were likewise decorated with these feathers, most profusely, according to Reid, on the eighth day, and when there was no more room on the walls the remaining feathers were added to the personal adornments of the dancers. One of J. P. Harrington's informants had a grandfather named *Tovemotar*, a very rich man and undoubtedly a clan leader, who had owned five of these banners. The ritual use of a painted pole, believed to represent the spirit of the person mourned, was observed at San Fernando, where it was called *kotumit*.

A sequence was recorded in 1922 by Benedict of a Serrano group, during which the first days of the mourning ceremony were spent in preparation, spiritual and material. The clan leader went into retreat with the sacred bundle, while ordinary folk prepared quantities of meal or took part in a rabbit drive. An all-night ceremony began on the third evening. The people assembled, and while they were singing the *paha* directed that all lights should be put out. Then he began to sing of the creation in a strange tone, and in ceremonial language. It was during this hour that the feathers were brought from their secret hiding places, and when the fires were rekindled the walls of the enclosure were decorated. At this time it was customary for the *paha* and other initiates to dance with the feathers, but Benedict was told that no one knew that dance any more, and besides the feathers were wearing out and had to be handled with great care.

On the fourth day the *paha* brought to the chief, one by one, the children who had been born during the year, and on each was bestowed a name from his father's lineage. This was one of the many occasions on which gifts were distributed. Sometimes they followed the custom, which seems to us an oddity, of throwing the gifts of shell money and seeds in the general direction of the recipients—who no doubt found some recreation in the ensuing scramble.

Images of the dead were made during the afternoon of the fifth day either by the relatives of those being mourned or by other people paid by them. In olden times these had consisted of narrow figures about five feet in length, made of rushes and draped with deerskin or twine skirts and decorated with feathers and beads. Later a wooden frame was substituted and white man's clothing was used for the covering. Images representing men were accompanied by bows and arrows, while those of the women bore baskets decorated with eagle feathers.

It was on this fifth day, probably at night, that the Eagle-killing ceremony was carried out. This was reported to have been held, in some groups, in honor of a dead chief, but it was deeply rooted in the religious philosophy and may have been held simply in honor of the eagle itself. The Luiseños said that the rite was first held after the death of *Wiyot*.

The Mission-trained Indians of Hugo Reid's day felt embarrassed when questioned about the status of the eagle in the native religion. Some would admit at once that the eagle had been their god, as though to silence the mocking curiosity of the inquirer, but Reid was told in good faith that the yearly rites had been held in honor of a remarkably clever and industrious chief, "who, when dying, told his people that he intended becoming an eagle, and that he bequeathed them his feathers, from henceforth to be employed at their feasts and ceremonies."

Among the Desert Cahuilla the eagles' nests which belonged to a given clan were kept under close observation and constantly guarded. A dance was held to celebrate the laying of the eggs, and as soon as the young birds grew their feathers five or six men went out to bring one or more of the eaglets to the owner, the clan chief. The chosen bird was carefully reared, and when it had achieved its full plumage a great "fiesta" was prepared. Hugo Reid did not include the feast held in honor of the eagle in his description of the Gabrielino mourning ceremony, but lists it as a separate event.

Among all these groups, whether the ceremony was as an independent ceremony or was given as one of the rites of the mourning observance, the fate of the captive eagle was the same. During the dance it was passed from hand to hand, each exerting a fervent pressure which gradually crushed the luckless victim. A final release was administered by one who knew how to press its heart to stillness. Not a drop of blood was supposed to be shed during this act of sacrifice, and with great reverence the body was skinned and the feathers added to the store of ceremonial costumes and decorations, while the carcass was ceremonially buried. The clan of Desert Cahuilla, mentioned above, rubbed the skin until it was very soft, and it, too, became a part of the sacred possessions of the clan leader, carefully rolled in a mat of rushes from the lagoons by the distant ocean.

As recorded by Father Boscana, the yearly bird feast concerned a girl who went away into the mountains where she met *Chungichnish* and was transformed by him into the *Panes*, translated as "White-headed Eagle Maiden." The description of the bird which Boscana saw in the ceremony at San Juan Capistrano is that of the California condor, rather than of an eagle, and it seems that this bird shared the veneration given to both the golden and the white-headed eagle.

No shadow of doubt crossed the minds of celebrants or onlookers that the *Panes* was reincarnated after each of these annual deaths. It seems to have been considered that the same bird figured in each and every one of these ceremonies, year after year, village by village. The introduction of this feminine figure, *Panes*, apparently a local one since elsewhere she is not mentioned, appears to be a rare intrusion into the predominantly masculine pantheon of the Shoshonean tribes. Even the moon, which in most ancient religions is a goddess, is here associated with *Wiyot*, though he seems to have been mourned as was this Eagle Maiden with never-assuaged grief and tears. The race held at the time of the appearance of each new moon carries the suggestion of a belief in rebirth, as does the conviction that the eagle lived again.

To return to the outline of an actual sequence of events recorded of one group of Serranos, a second eagle dance occurred on the sixth day. This was the athletic, whirling movement which the Luiseños called the *morahash*, and the Diegueños the *tatahuilla*. No actual bird figured in this event. The men who performed it, each taking his turn for a solo performance amid a swirl of the long eagle feathers which formed the fringe of the net dance skirts, had been chosen to learn it at the time of their initiation during boyhood, because of outstanding swiftness and grace displayed on that occasion. In fact, this dance seems to have been associated with the cult of initiation and it is unknown among such groups as the Desert Cahuilla, who had a mourning ceremony but were beyond the orbit of the cult of initiation of boys.

About an hour before dawn on the seventh day, after a night of singing, the images were brought out, either by a woman of the dead person's clan but not closely related to him, or by a woman of another clan who was paid for her services. For perhaps half an hour the images were carried in the dance and then were thrown into a great bonfire which had been kindled in an open space.

Images of this sort were called by the personal names of the deceased and after the burning they were not supposed to be mentioned again, but since lineage names were bestowed in succeeding generations they had a sort of immortality of their own. It is probable that gifts had been sent from near and far, relayed along, to the chief in whose clan the death had occurred. If so, these were returned to the donors at the conclusion of the great ceremonies, at the time of the distribution of other gifts and fees.

In all of these ceremonies there came a time when the property of the deceased which had been reserved at the time of his death was brought to the fire and destroyed. Metates were broken and holes were knocked into the bottoms of mortars. Baskets and other more perishable possessions went into the flames. Needless to say, many archeological discoveries in this area consist of accumulations of material found in pits, the evidences of charcoal and the "killed" grinding stones recalling the final scenes of these rites, when the fires which had been kept blazing by the descendant of *Toovit*, Brush Rabbit, were finally put out and the earth packed down over those who had been mourned.

When a fully initiated person died the services of the *Takwa*, the "eater" and official "Divider of Food," were called into play. In commemoration of the act of Coyote, who seized a portion of flesh from the body of *Wiyot* as it lay on the funeral pyre, this man was supposed to consume some flesh from the shoulder of the dead celebrity. The hearts of the notables who were honored in this way were believed to take their places in the sky as stars, while ordinary folk went to an underworld where they made merry with dancing and feasting. The very last event of the memorial observances for such an important man, a final farewell, took place when his feather headdress was buried in a hole in the center of a ground-painting, a hole which itself represented the entrance to a world beyond this one.

In Mission times, when the impact of European civilization had made these Indians feel that there was something not quite respectable in some of their ancient practices, they began to hide certain of them from foreign eyes, or to modify them, and at last almost to forget just how they had been performed in the long ago. Thus, even now among the Luiseños, the last initiates, now middle-aged men, still dance with feather head-tufts topping their modern clothing. One by one, down to some final time in the foreseeable future, these headdresses are buried in the center of a ground-painting. Then occurs the rite of washing and burning the clothing of the dead, a not very spectacular performance which probably has its roots deep in the rather weird practices of that powerful figure, the *Takwa*.

Most probably inspired by the belief that to swallow something of the essence of the dead person would be to receive some of his power, there had been an ancient custom of giving to the bereaved relatives a drink compounded of a small portion of the burned and powdered bones of the deceased, saved from the cremation and mixed with water. The rite of washing the clothing may have been a substitute for this, since often a ceremonial drink is taken from the water in which these are washed. Some groups mix a little meal made from "chia" seed with the water. Later the clothing is burned. The timing of these acts varies with the locality, just as in earlier days the events which made up the great mourning ceremony were celebrated in differing localities with a bewildering number of variations and in differing order, although the underlying concepts appear to have been identical.

Father Boscana found the dances which he witnessed monotonous but generally decent, with the exception of one during which first a man and then a woman danced alone, the latter singing to the accompaniment of a bone flute a song naively enumerating rather obvious details of her anatomical structure. The dance costumes seemed to him somewhat drab, and compared with the bright plumage and colorful masks employed by some other tribes this observation holds good. The simple top-knot of owl or hawk feathers and the skirt fringed with long, dark eagle feathers were less a matter of adornment than a uniform costume for initiates engaged in the worship of a great and solemn figure. Brighter hues seem more often associated with lesser spirits and gods. The naked men, squatting for long hours to watch the continually repeated steps of the dancers, did indeed appear ridiculous to the cultivated European eye, but the richness of the song-texts and the capacity for contemplation of deeply inward images, no matter how crudely and even barbarically expressed, must be recognized. This was the unique genius of the Gabrielino Indians.

Dance steps observed in modern times among the related tribes are of three main types: the swiftly whirling *morahash*, already mentioned, the fire dance in which a large number of barefooted performers extinguished a blazing bonfire, and the formation called *hortloi* by the Diegueños, whose accompanying songs were in the Gabrielino language. In the fire dance, as each man took his turn for a momentary but determined advance into the blaze, he pushed as much dirt ahead of him as he could manage, but nevertheless the effort and the effect were spectacular in the extreme. The *hortloi* was a typical Indian circling movement accomplished by a forward jump with both feet, followed by a long step, and varied by stamping in place and backward jumps. Americans have called this a war dance, but Kroeber says it appears to have no reference to war.

To have allowed the extensive literature of the Gabrielino ceremonies to have been lost is one of the tragedies of ignorance. Charles Lummis, founder of the Southwest Museum and early apostle of the values to be found in the primitive cultures of our predecessors on this continent, did capture some Gabrielino singing on an early type of cylindrical phonograph record, and for the collection of Luiseño recordings in the Museum of the University of California, Constance Goddard Du Bois was able to translate texts.

Definite poetic and mythological themes recur throughout the texts recorded by Du Bois, but the phrasing and the melodies appear to have been individual, the properties of the prolific composers, certain persons or clans. Some were in the nature of recitatives, and it would appear that the feeling ranged from the sweet and plaintive to the strong and dramatic. There existed an infinite number of songs for occasions such as the need of the shamans to assure good harvests of acorns and seeds, to bring rainfall, or to curse or bless enemies or friends. For the extended rituals there were long song-cycles on such subjects as death, the seasons, the spirit, the First People, landmarks which once had been people, and the *Chungichnish* avengers.

Transcriptions of Luiseño, Gabrielino and Catalineño songs are to be found in the book, "Form in Primitive Music," by Helen H. Roberts. Fortune favored both musicologists and anthropologists in that this particular author was able to find informants who still could provide such authentic material for her analysis.

Some of the songs of this collection deal with Creation, the death of *Wiyot* (woyo'te), mourning rites, deer killing. Others seem to have no ceremonial connection. One tells of a clan which migrated from Santa Catalina to the Luiseño shore. Wild geese, bees, and "the little, white seagull" appeared at their camp on

The Boy's Vision, from "Yamino Kwiti," by Donna Preble. (Courtesy Caxton Printers).

the mainland. Encouraged by these favorable signs they remained, thus displacing a more timid clan of Luiseños, which wandered until it found a permanent home farther inland.

A song of Gabrielino origin was of a type, the informant said, which was like praying. "The spirit of the person who died went away through a gate in the east, early in the morning when it was not yet light, to do thereafter 'whatever the angels wished'." These excerpts give only a hint of the value of Roberts' work in this field.

Connected with the ritual that grew from the *Chungichnish* religion was a cult of initiation for the males. This seems, at least in some groups, to have been held whenever there was a large enough crop of young aspirants, even though some quite sleepy little fellows found themselves kneeling with the somewhat older boys as they drank from the large, ceremonial mortar in which a drink had been made from the dried, pounded root of the jimson weed, called *manit* by the Gabrielinos. This is now known as the toloache cult, the word being borrowed by the Spanish from the Aztec *toloatzin*, applied to a plant of the Datura family. The jimson weed is classified by botanists as *Datura meteloides.*

The drink was highly intoxicating and as the dancing of that first night progressed the boys, one by one, fell into a stupor. Laid in a secluded place, each boy was watched throughout his long sleep by an adult male who may have been his sponsor. During his stupor the lad had visions which were to remain with him throughout his life as a special relationship between himself and the supernatural. A specific animal which appeared in such a vision became for the dreamer a sort of guardian spirit, although Kroeber, commenting on the Luiseño cult, says it would be misleading to name the practice as being outright "shamanistic" or "totemic."

Father Boscana mentions a three-day fast at this time and tells of other youths who fasted for a similar time in the *Wamkich* without partaking of the intoxicating toloache. These were adorned with feathers and painted black and red, and for them a ground-painting was made, a "most uncouth and ridiculous figure of an animal." If, as this seems to imply, there were two classes of initiates, the ones who did not partake of the toloache may have been of higher rank, but it is more probable that they were in later stages of initiation, having at an earlier time suffered the initial fast and the vision-haunted sleep.

It would be impossible to reconstruct the Gabrielino time sequence for the events which made up the toloache rite. There is a wide variance in the practices of the groups which took it over. Among the Luiseños all of the candidates were present at the making of the ground-painting and during the lectures on its symbolism, as well as while listening to the extended instruction on the duties of an adult, which accompanied this phase.

In another part of the rite Luiseño boys were required to leap from stone to stone of a row of three which had been laid in a narrow trench amid the meshes of a net of milkweed fiber. The net was shaped to represent the human figure and the song texts referred to the fibers as human hair, symbolic of the spirit. The Luiseño name was one of their characteristic ceremonial couplets, *wanal wanawut* or *yula wanawut*, meaning spirit and net, and there was more than a hint of a passage through the grave in this rite. In fact each boy was watched with anxiety as a slip meant the certainty of an early death. The hazard was real, as he was required to perform the leaps in a crouching posture while still undergoing the fast which accompanied the toloache drinking.

Among the Luiseños the fast was complete at first, then relaxed to the point of allowing unsalted mush. The days and weeks went by, the candidates sleeping by day and dancing by night. Gradually the fast was relaxed and a return made to normal procedures, but not until a month or two had passed did the boys take off the belts which had eased the pangs of their hunger and join a race to the *Wamkich*. This burst of unregulated energy contrasted sharply with the slow animal

A Gabrielino ceremonial dance as visualized by Donna Preble,
author and artist, in her book "Yamino-Kwiti." (Courtesy Caxton
Printers, Ltd.)

crawl, the "fantastical procession" observed by Father
Boscana, which, during the first days of the rite, they
had copied from their elders as the correct approach to
the sacred shrine.

If it were not for the very few Luiseños who have been able to recall some of the ancient ground-paintings we would have very little idea of this art as it was practiced by the Gabrielinos. Although the work appears to have been sketchy in comparison to this form of painting as it has been developed by the Indians of the Southwest, the origin of it is probably to be found in ancient contact with the early Pueblo people, long before the Shoshonean migrations into California. The Luiseño paintings contained symbolic portrayals of such objects and concepts as the Milky Way, the Night, the Sky, human blood, arms, the spirit, the *Chungich-nish* avengers. Always in the center of a circular painting was a hole which typified death and the hereafter, and the circle itself represented the "whole world."

Father Boscana tells of an enterprising youth who, left alone in the *Wamkich*, secretly crept out and violated his fast and even injured with his foot a portion of the sacred painting. Finding himself still alive led to boasting of his exploit to the other teen-agers, which in turn led to his immediate execution. His elders took a dim view of such revolutionary experiments. For such an execution the chief was not obliged to soil his hands, or even to give a definite order. It was easy to work his clansmen into a holy fury simply by having a crier go forth to tell the tale and warn of the consequences. Before long the whole village had become one united vigilante committee with but a single thought.

The instruction which accompanied the ritual activities of the initiations seemed principally to be directed toward the maintenance of a smooth social regime. The displeasure and the vengeance of *Chungichnish* fell, it seemed, on those who failed in respect, obedience and generosity toward their elders, or who were greedy, as typified by secret, nocturnal eating of food which had been put by for breakfast. The darker and more violent sins were not mentioned, probably because they were too obvious, although Reid said that robbery was unknown among them and that murder was rare.

As a part of their preparation for adulthood young men were tested and hardened by methods that seem quite extreme. They were whipped with nettles and stung by myriads of red ants, sometimes while lying in a disturbed nest of those aggressive insects. Music from a deerbone flute and dancing by the men added a festive note to the observance. The conclusion of this period was attested by a branding, usually on the upper right arm. A patch of dry, highly combustible leaves of the California mugwort was set on fire, raising a large blister. A scar resulted and any male who went through life without this sign was considered to be a weakling and utterly unfit.

Among the Serranos the toloache ceremony was held only for boys of prominent families or who showed unusual promise. The *Paha* was assisted by shamans and the drink was administered to the youths in a secret place outside the village. In the subsequent dance in the ceremonial enclosure one boy after another fell into a stupor in which he was allowed to lie until the effects of the drug wore off. On the third day all the boys ran a race and the winner was chosen to be the one trained for the whirling eagle dance.

Strong was told, also, of the use of toloache as it was carried out by the clans of the Mountain Cahuilla. Here the *manet* plant was said to mean "grass that could talk," a speech, however, that could only be heard by the shamans. *Manet* "belonged to the water," and the ritual songs were in the "ocean language." This was probably Gabrielino, since we know that some ceremonial songs even among the Luiseños and Diegueños are conceded to be in this tongue and as little understood as "ocean language" was by the Cahuilla.

Kroeber includes the religious use of the jimson weed with those elements of Shoshonean culture which extend back into ancient times before the migration into California, but says, "The definite cult, however, in which the plant is employed, the mythology with which it is brought into relation, the ritual actions and songs that constitute its body, were worked out primarily if not wholly by the Gabrielino." The toloache was used but once in the initiation ceremonies and very seldom in a non-ritual fashion. The Palm Springs Cahuilla sometimes chewed the leaves as a narcotic, and Kroeber reports that the drink, mixed with salt water, was used by the Gabrielinos to "give strength, inpenetrability to arrows, immunity from bear and snake bites, and fortune in the hunt."

At the conclusion of the Luiseño rites the sacred enclosure, at least in ancient times, was burned. All the signs of the event were destroyed, lest an unauthorized person should observe them. The *wanawut* trench had been filled, covering the net, as the last boy completed his passage through it. At the conclusion of the period of instruction connected with the ground-painting each boy had been given a lump of sage meal and salt which he put in his mouth, and, kneeling, spat into the central hole of the painting, the symbolic entrance to *tolmal*, the lower world of the hereafter. Into a similar hole in another painting the headdress, which he was now entitled to wear, would be buried in the time of his mourning; but now, still young and eagerly alive, he watched the symbolic mouthful of sage and salt disappear as the old seers shoved the pigments into the opening and packed the earth down over the last signs of the painting. The sacred mortar used in brewing the *manit* drink was buried until the time when another crop of young aspirants should mature.

The toloache cult spread into neighboring tribes at about the time it was being abandoned by its Gabrielino originators, as they became largely absorbed into the life of the Franciscan Missions. Within the history of the puberty ceremonies of these people it seems to mark a late phase, since it was well organized and had a definite theological basis. Far older and closer to their earliest rites were those connected with the three great mysteries of birth, death and girl's puberty. These are so universal among hunting and gathering Indians that Ruth Underhill believes them "to have been brought from Asia itself."

Possibly in the remote past menstruation seemed awesome, even dangerous and malignant, and at its first appearance the fear of it was intensified. Only after the boy's ceremony became highly developed did the more ancient rite for girls become outranked in importance. The Gabrielinos, who possessed a complicated theology and a boy's ritual, still celebrated the girl's puberty rite, but not as a protection from malignant forces. For them it was rather in the nature of a début, a joyous presentation to society of a marriageable young woman.

Old taboos such as not eating meat and scratching the head with a stick instead of fingers remained, but the main concern in the girl's ritual was for her health and future happiness. These they tried to ensure by practically baking her in a pit, protected from a bed of hot stones by an aromatic mattress of the branches of such plants as the California mugwort and the western ragweed.

Such a ceremony must have been a startling event in the life of a young Indian girl, contrasting sharply with an obscure childhood of dawn plunges into cold pools, cold food and scant protection from inclement weather. Although she must fast for the three days she spent in the perhaps too warm luxury of the heated pit, she drank and was bathed in warm water and was the central figure of hours of dancing and singing and distribution of gifts and food.

Among the Luiseños the ceremony for a girl at the time of puberty began with a test of her virtue. If she could swallow and retain a ball of tobacco this was proved; if she regurgitated society formed an adverse opinion. During her fast in the heated pit, so suggestive of a grave except for its warmth, she could leave it only once in 24 hours while the stones were being reheated. An open-work basket was laid over her face and she was supposed to be utterly motionless during her rest. After three days her face was painted by the wife of the visiting official in charge of the ceremony, and anklets and bracelets of human hair and shell necklaces were placed on her person. Food restrictions were continued for some time and could be voluntarily observed for a year or longer.

A ground-painting was made for the girl's ceremony and explained by the *paha*. For them, as for the boys, moral lectures were given, telling them how to conduct themselves in order to be popular socially and avoid the calamities that awaited anyone who annoyed the ever-watchful *Chungichnish*. A girl must be industrious and never a gadabout; she must remember to bathe daily, to be hospitable, and have a straightforward manner without deceit. She, too, took into her mouth at the end of the ceremony a ball of sage meal and salt, spat it into the central hole of the ground-painting, then watched as the painting itself followed into that symbolic pit and the earth was packed down above it.

Usually, in order to economize on the fees of the officials and the considerable amounts of food and gifts that were required for such an affair, several girls received the honor at once, even though only one had actually reached puberty at that particular time. After the ground-painting was destroyed the girls' faces were painted and then all ran a race to a designated rock, where either the girls themselves or the wife of the official in charge made a large geometric painting. This phase of the ceremony, face-painting, race, and rock-painting, was repeated each month for a short period. Vestiges of these designs, done in sheltered places, are still to be found.

Reid described the Gabrielino ceremony held for mothers after childbirth. It was somewhat like the one held for the girls, as for three days the woman was subjected to steaming over an aperture leading from a pit filled with extremely hot rocks on which water was thrown. Her fast was complete except for warm water and was concluded by the ritual swallowing of three pills made of meat and tobacco. Intercourse was not resumed between husband and wife until after the child was weaned.

By tradition a man felt deeply identified with the condition of his wife, particularly in the days immediately preceding and following the birth. It was customary for him to observe a fast from salt, meat and grease, and to neither fish nor hunt. Among certain tribes of South America the taboos of this period were so numerous there was very little left for a man to do

but take to his hammock and sleep. Similar customs
have been observed in practically every quarter of the
globe and seem to occupy a phase in which a matri-
linear system is changing to the patrilinear. It has
even been reported from Corsica and Albania, and with
less certainty from early Basque and Celtic groups. The
European term used to designate such a practice is the
"couvade."

Father Boscana criticizes severely the lax upbringing
of the young and then goes on to describe the rather
severe deprivations suffered by boys and girls, up to
and even following the birth of the first child to a
young couple. Babies were welcomed and petted and
whipping was unknown as a method of discipline, but
quite early a child learned that the places by the fire
belonged to his elders, that deer meat was not for him,
that one did not pass between two adults who might be
conversing, or even hang about and listen to what they
said. Etiquette was extremely involved. One might
joke with relatives or members of certain clans and not
with others, and no boy might call his sister a liar,
even in jest. Punishment for infringement of any one
of dozens of such delicate matters lay in the hands of
the avengers of *Chungichnish*, but a really incorrigible
boy might actually be liquidated by an aroused citizenry and his family made to feel the weight of the dis-
grace.

As to education, each child must learn to take his
place in a society where every material need had to be
met from the raw materials found in mountain, thicket,
plain, pool and sea. Beyond the necessary skills he must
acquire for these needs came the memorizing of myths,
song cycles and ritual sequences, for all those who
would grow up to participate in the ceremonial activities, or to administer and pass on the law and the lore
of the people.

Certain men who possessed the mental and manual
alertness required of a shaman attained to great power
and esteem. The *paha* was an outstanding individual
from this profession, and we may imagine that small
boys were closely observed to single out those who

showed aptitude. It is possible that these brighter young-
sters found themselves sponsored during their toloache
rites by the men who planned to take them on as their
successors in the practice of magical and curative arts.
Such a boy may have been touched on the neck or
chest by his sponsor's own sacred talisman, or may have
been given something to swallow which he knew came
from the heart of the old shaman, although it appeared
to come from his mouth.

Reid transcribed the name for the tribal "medical
men" as *a-hub-su-voi-rot* and this name, with quite a
different spelling, appears in a Gabrielino vocabulary
procured at a later date. Another name for shaman was
pul, the plural being *pupulam*. The Palm Springs Cahuilla reported two kinds of shamans, the *pul*, or curing
doctor, and those who had the ability to turn themselves into bears. Of the Gabrielinos we know only
that they did have "bear doctors." Both names, however applied in olden times, were translated into Spanish as "hechicero," or wizard, and whatever specialties
each type possessed, shamans as a class had no little
knowledge of the healing arts. The list of plant material for which these men knew curative uses runs to a
considerable length and should not be discounted as
the more startling aspects of their practice come to
light.

In general therapy they not only used the herbal
preparations, but set up counter-irritations in the forms
of whipping with nettles, scarifying the flesh with
sharp bits of flint, or allowing ants to bite the affected
part. Steaming and blood-letting were accepted methods.
A *pul*, however, could kill as well as cure, knew how to
mesmerize a patient, and had a whole kit of sleight-of-
hand tricks to hold the people spellbound and ensure his
power over them. He possessed "second sight" and
could tell at a glance the moral and physical condition
of any person on whom he turned his searching glance.

The power of a shaman came to him directly from
the supernatural, through dreams and visions beginning
possibly with those seen during the toloache rite, but
it had been fostered by his teacher and by no lack of

industry on his own part. Although the mountain, the rock or the animal of which he had dreamed was replete with energizing power, it took amazing skill to put on a convincing exhibition of fire-handling or sword-swallowing. The Luiseños told of shamans who could cut off their tongues, show the bleeding member, and then return it to place perfectly whole, and of one *pul* shooting another with an arrow, only to pull the shaft free and restore the apparently dead colleague to life.

The theory was held that sickness was caused by the presence in the patient's body of some foreign object, often interjected by the malevolent action of another shaman. To remove this the *pul* sucked the part affected and then exhibited the recovered object as evidence of his success. He also might blow tobacco smoke toward the sufferer, using sacred pipes of soapstone. A malevolent shaman could send his magic from any distance to cause disease and death to a person he disliked. And though he spared his own patients and was believed to do his best for them, and so was not blamed or punished for mishaps to them, sometimes he came to his death through a general rebellion against the overweening power he exercised. Strong was told of the execution of a Cahuilla shaman who claimed to be God, could "catch bullets in his hand, pull up tobacco from the ground, and see the child in the sun." It was believed that he had bewitched and killed many people, and his own daughter asked the people to join in ending what seems a rather pathetic career.

Among the shamans there was always a primitive astronomer who could predict the return of the moon. From the information we have it would appear that regular months of 28 days were recognized, until midwinter and midsummer when the solstices occurred. These events made such an impression and were felt to be so important that they threw the whole lunar system out of kilter. The necessary adjustment of the calendar seems to have resulted in a year of 10 months, two of which were reckoned around the solstices in such a way that they contained an extra full moon. This lopsided arrangement was perfectly practical for men who cared nothing at all for recorded dates, and it was, moreover, a very ancient system which probably had served them before they ever saw California.

The Gabrielino names for their months are lost, but those recorded of the Luiseños by Du Bois were explained by delightfully descriptive phrases such as "the month of Tasmoymal, when the grass begins to grow green." This was April, and by its occurrence in the song cycles it proves to be the first month of the Luiseño year. June was described by the phrase "the eagles now fly," and October tells of "little streams of water washing the fallen leaves." In the name for December one is reminded that this is the season after the harvest, "When one gets padded out with fat all over one's body."

It is probable that the Gabrielinos distinguished between the "breath" and the "heart" as two concepts for the enduring elements, the latter coming closer to the western idea of the soul and the former corresponding to ghost. This was true particularly of the hearts of great men who had been honored by the ceremonial attention of the *Takwa*, the "Eater." The ghosts of lesser men might linger awhile, unseen, at last to go to an abode of which Father Boscana's informants did not seem sure—perhaps because if they told him of *Tolmal*, the underworld, he might confuse it with the western idea of hell. Fear of the return of the newly dead could be capitalized upon by shamans, who used it to prey on superstitious, fearful women.

A great comet in the sky meant the passage of a good and noble chief to his abode among the planets, or perhaps his return to earth. *Tacu*, the comet (no relation to the "Eater," or to *Takwis*), was in some versions of the Creation Myth a parent of *Chungichnish*. The "little stars," the Pleiades, were maidens, while falling stars were "children of the moon" and not only indicated a death in the group but could make any woman who looked at one disfigured and ugly. The morning and the evening stars were *jo'ojt sijot*, the "Big Stars," and Polaris was "the star that does not move." The

Luiseños had names for the important stars and knew them as chiefs among the "First People" of long ago. For them the Milky Way was the Spirit and the home of the spirits of mankind. It seems clear that we know the mere vestiges of the star lore of these people and of the religious symbolism and philosophical concepts connected with it.

A rainbow was the sign of good fortune, while an eclipse was greeted as an unmitigated calamity, with shouting, weeping and pounding with sticks on the ground, on hides or on tule mats. It was believed that some monster was swallowing the heavenly body. Sometimes songs were sung to "help the moon get well." Lightning may have been considered to be the "eye of thunder," while ball lightning was connected with *Takwis*. J. P. Harrington believes that reference to meteors or falling stars as associated with this dreaded figure is incorrect.

"These people were not entirely destitute of any knowledge of the universal deluge, but how or from whence they received the same, I could never understand," wrote Father Boscana. "Some of their songs refer to it, and they have a tradition that, at a time very remote, the sea began to swell and roll in upon the plains, and fill the valleys, until it had covered the mountains; and thus nearly all the human race and animals were destroyed, excepting a few who had resorted to a very high mountain which the waters did not reach."

For the Luiseños the "high mountain" was a little knoll near Bonsall which the Spanish called "Mora" and the Indians *Katuta*. Although the hill has been measured and found to be 940 feet in altitude the Indians believed it grew higher during the period of the emergency. This is also another of the many landmarks which had been one of the "First People." The Gabrielino name for this hill was *Katukta* and they said the people there ate mud as the water rose.

The owl announced the impending death of some person nearby with his hooting, the humming bird by falling down dead beside one. The crow advised when a stranger was approaching, but the raven was no ordinary indicator of events, but an important figure in the long list of the animals, birds, insects and inanimate objects which were sacred to *Chungichnish* and could act as his avengers. Du Bois, writing of the Luiseños, says "The raven was the special messenger of *Chungichnish* and was able to tell the secret transgressions of those who offended against him, revealed the secrets, made mistakes in ceremonies, or disobeyed the rules of life; but it was not everyone who could hear what the raven said. It was only the shamans of greatest power, those who could hear and see everything and kill a person at a distance."

A major work of listing the creatures which are known to have been sacred to *Chungichnish* is to be found in John Peabody Harrington's annotations to Robinson's translation of "Chinigchinich" by Fr. Boscana, published by the Fine Arts Press of Santa Ana, California. Among them were Raven, who was also *Tukupar*, the Sky, and the whole eagle and hawk family. Those and many others contributed their beaks and talons to the sacred bundle, where also were to be found the mountain lion's claws. Rattlesnakes, black widow spiders, tarantulas, and even the blackberry bushes and the wild roses, since they grew thorns that could scratch, belonged to this category. Strangest of all were the minerals which were invested with life and personality and deep esoteric power.

Tosaut, the rock that Father Boscana mentions as having been used to anchor the world at the time of creation and as having contained the gall that made the sea salty, seems to have been, in Chumash country, a black basalt found on Santa Barbara Island, but the sacred fragments found near San Juan Capistrano may have been of another mineral. Clear rock crystals were said by the Luiseños to be the arrows of the sacred raven and to cause internal pains. Tourmaline crystals were rubbed on the bodies of the sick as a cure but any unauthorized person who touched one was punished and no one went hunting for them without due ceremonial preparation and prayer.

David Banks Rogers, during his intensive excavations of sites in Ventura and Santa Barbara counties, found two clusters of the famous cigar-shaped "charm stones" which were cut from stone not native to the region. They varied in size from nearly two inches to more than 13 in length and from 3/16ths of an inch in diameter to one and one-half. These had been laid in a circle "radiating from a central circular piece that was encircled by a band of asphaltum and rested in a small cup-shaped boulder like a golf-ball in a tee." In 1928 Rogers visited in the hills behind Tehachapi an old Indian believed to be the son of Canaliño Indians who had run away from the Santa Barbara Mission in 1824. When he showed "Old George" one of these charm stones the Indian instantly turned his back, shouting a warning to Rogers: "Don't look at it. It may not be dead."

The explanation which "Old George" gave was that such stones are alive and burrow in the ground like moles. To look at one would cause serious illness, perhaps paralysis. Only a medicine man could capture one and only he knew how to kill it. Once dead, however, such a stone would bring its owner good fortune and an Indian would pay well for it.

Many other objects were sacred, such as the mortar and the baskets which were used to make the toloache drink, and the pipes of the shamans. Certain perforated round stones that have been found in Gabrielino sites, decorated with feathers and hafted on slender sticks, must have had a ceremonial use but it is not known. Shamans carried *paviut* sticks or wands, flaring at the top, decorated with haliotis shell and tipped with a flint knife or a rock crystal, and initiates were given similar wands without the knives or crystals. The shaman wore a board, painted red and decorated with snake rattles held upright against his forehead with a feathered band, whenever he undertook to make rain or to show his powers of magic. A feathered slat was bound to the forehead of a new chief with a cord of human hair.

Even paint had an involved ceremonial significance.

Ceremonial wands or "paviut sticks". (Courtesy Riverside Municipal Museum).

Among the Luiseños the word *paha* means "red racer snake," and as the female of that species is black and the male red, the *paha* painted himself red on one side of his body and black on the other. The Cupeño and some other tribes used a striped pattern for the members of the coyote moiety and spots to distinguish the wildcat party. This gives only a faint hint as to the numerous expressions of a basic twofold ordering of the society which might be found.

Drums are absent from the list of musical instruments used by these tribes. Split-stick clappers, clusters of cocoons attached to a stick handle, and turtle shell rattles were rhythm instruments, as were bunches of deer hooves attached by thongs or cords to a short stick. A bull-roarer made its whizzing noise for amusement and during the toloache fire dances. There were whistles of bird bone and of cane, and flutes of deer bone and elder wood, the stops treated with asphalt.

For amusements there were endless variations of the cat's cradle, archery practice using little bunches of tule thrown at moving targets, and a lively hoop and pole game employing a tule hoop. Hugo Reid enumerated and described quite a variety of gambling games, including the one which became famous under its Spanish name of "peon."

In addition to the myths and legends connected with their religion the Gabrielinos also told fables and legends that might be classified under the heading of amusing fiction, although one of the several which were recorded by Reid has a characteristic religious theme of a girl who conceived a child by supernatural means, in this case by falling in love with the lightning. Her name, *Chukit*, appears in a roster of supernatural beings among the Fernandeños and probably is the same as the Yokuts goddess, *Tsukit*.

Kroeber quotes in his "Handbook" one of the secular stories transcribed by Hugo Reid and comments, as did the collector, on its extravagant and illogical plot. It contains, he points out, such "ethical inconsistencies" that we are revolted by it. So many contradictions crop up, one after the other, that he feels the originators were not striving to construct a plot at all, but rather to build up an effect of "deliberate or artistic incoherence."

This quality, so characteristic of the mythology of the tribes of Southern California, is not due to an absence of aesthetic feeling but, to use Kroeber's words, is "rather an evidence of subtle refinement of emotion, of decorative over-elaboration of some literary quality, to such a degree that the ordinary rules of satisfaction and balance and moral proportion become inconsequential . . . . . Most likely, as among the Mohave, stories like this one are little else than a web that carries a rich embroidery of songs, which yield their own emotional stimulus, and at the same time endow the plot, when sensed through their medium, with a brilliant and profound luminousness that makes immaterial the presence or absence of anything else."

In our time, when the primitive is felt to be fascinating and picturesque, Indian ceremonials tend to be regarded as mere theatrical performances. The lack of knowledge of their underlying meaning on the part of the eager viewers, together with the hasty tempo and the competitive pressure of modern life, tend to devalue for the Indian himself the heritage from his more leisurely past. In Father Boscana's time, and in Hugo Reid's, the separation from their roots in nature had already begun for the Gabrielinos. We owe to these two men, and to the later investigators among the related tribes, all that we can glean of the subtle and poetic veil of imagery through which these people viewed their inner, subjective world, and with which the daily life of each of them was so mystically interwoven. We have John Peabody Harrington to thank for the preservation of a phrase which sounds as though it might have been the first tenet in a Gabrielino's statement of his religious faith, *"Tavi hetekrinuj atavin tuvangnar,"* —"God has placed the whole world."

The Seacoast
and the
Rivers

Along the ocean shore of their own homeland the Gabrielino villages teemed with well-fed fishermen and their thriving families. The kitchen-middens, or ancient refuse heaps, which mark these forgotten sites are like all coastal village remains, deep, darkened with innumerable bits of charcoal from old fires, and with a telltale oiliness that adds its own evidence to the myriads of fishbones and broken shells.

Most of these middens, as well as the burial grounds, have long since been robbed of their mortars and pestles, of their fine chert and obsidian arrow points and knives, of their exquisitely shaped fish hooks of haliotis shell, by casual or commercial souvenir hunters of a day long before such activities earned from the systematic archeologist the contemptuous term "pot-hunting." Because such amateur excavations have forever destroyed or scattered valuable clues in regard to ancient man the federal government and some states now prohibit them on lands within their jurisdiction.

Mainland woman trading with islanders. (Drawing by Allen W. Welts).

In the heydays of these coastal settlements men came to them from the inland villages to barter for dried fish and shell, no doubt bringing deer hides and perhaps acorns and "chia" seeds to exchange. Clamshell beads were used as currency in trading. From Santa Catalina Island, in the great plank canoes, came prized objects of steatite: cooking pots, ceremonial bowls and pipes, fine little carvings of animals, fish, and birds, and blocks of the raw stone for the use of artisans on the mainland. The islands could offer, as well, the precious sea-otter skins. We cannot altogether imagine what the mainland could supply to match these riches, but the wide dispersal of the steatite objects bears witness to a brisk trade.

The river valleys, too, were dotted with rancherias,

their locations chosen with an eye to the vagrant habits of the streams. Not even an Indian, however, could always outguess such prima donnas as those temperamental rivers which the Spanish were finally to name the Santa Ana de los Temblores, the San Gabriel, and the Porciuncula, the latter in honor of Our Lady, the Queen of the Angels of Porciuncula, which was the name to be given to the tiny pueblo which would one day be founded near the river bank.

Many years later, following the floods of 1914, when it became obvious that these streams must yield to a civilizing restraint, interviews were held with the old settlers still able to recall the storms of earlier decades. The report thus gathered could compete in suspense with mystery fiction, as one after another of these long-time residents told which way the waters ran after too copious winter rains, such as those of 1814, '24, '51, '67, '87, and '89. From it we learn what to us is startling information. With few exceptions old residents recalled that, until the floods of 1824-25 sent it careening off through the lowlands to the south, the Los Angeles River ran below a high bluff between the present Main and Los Angeles Streets, turning westward on its meandering way to the "cienegas," the great marshlands that lay between the Baldwin and the Beverly hills. This course can be traced roughly today by observing the trend of the low ground in the region of Venice, Adams and Washington, between La Brea and La Cienega Boulevards, in the present city of Los Angeles.

From some unknown prior date, or perhaps always until the winter of 1824-25, this was the course the Los Angeles River followed to its mouth in the Santa Monica Bay. Thereafter, during every major storm, until a deep, concrete-lined channel formed a strait-jacket for its deceptive strength, this was the way it threatened to take and deep sands exist to prove its right to such a course. "The river needed to rise only a few inches to send it down the old channel," reported one old resident. In 1867 this actually happened and for a while the water stood like a great lake all the way to the "cienegas." From that point to the sea the course had been that of the stream the Spanish were to call "La Ballona," although the low ground southward to the Dominguez country sometimes coaxed the overflow in that direction.

La Ballona's upper reaches are now tucked away underground and it emerges for its last few miles as a mere creek with straight and unlovely concrete banks. Its present exit to the sea can only suggest the broad delta of those other days, when the drainage of the great San Fernando Valley came on a long, roundabout journey to merge with the flow from a myriad canyon rivulets and spring-fed brooks from the Hollywood, Beverly and Baldwin hills. Streams now long forgotten added their volume, like those which carried the overflow from the pools of the present MacArthur Park, or the "King's Waterway," sometimes called "San Juan de Reyes," which ran down Grand Avenue.

During the winter rains the swampy delta became a vast inland sea from the higher ground of Culver City to the ocean. The Gabrielinos called this by their general name for any bay, *pwinukipar*, meaning "it is full of water," but in summer they amended this to "the water has departed." Equally descriptive was the later Spanish name for the holding which antedated the present city of Beverly Hills, "Rancho Rodeo de las Aguas," the "Ranch of the Meeting of the Waters."

The San Gabriel River had its own dark history. It carried a great volume of the run-off from many a mountain canyon around by Azusa and then to the east of El Monte, "down Basset way," as old residents phrased it. From the pass which we call the Whittier Narrows it ran a long southwesterly course to empty into San Pedro Bay by a choice of exits in a wide fan. One of these coincided almost exactly with the mouth of the present Los Angeles River. The Rio Hondo of those days was a creek of only a couple of miles through which the overflow from the swamps below El Monte reached the San Gabriel. How the Rio Hondo fell heir to most of the sources and a considerable portion of the main channel of the parent stream, to become the principal tributary of the Los Angeles River,

Rivers of the Gabrielino country. (Map by Allen W. Welts).

is again a story of the vagaries of the winter storms and of disturbances of nature by ambitious white farmers.

Below the Whittier Narrows the low ground directly to the south had always formed a temptation to the fickle San Gabriel River. One early map is said to have shown it going that way, but tradition credits an irrigation ditch on the land of Don Pio Pico as the avenue through which the final plunge was made, during the flood of 1867. Thereafter it emptied into Alamitos Bay although other winter rains found it making temporary sallies in the direction of its abandoned bed. On some maps the southward flowing stream was called simply "New River." In 1869 a map for an early subdivision into small farms of the wide rancho lands shows the "New San Gabriel" going south to Alamitos while the "Old San Gabriel" follows its original course. The Los Angeles River is shown on this map as a tributary to the old San Gabriel, as indeed it should have been, being a mere interloper in that territory.

Across much of the land between the modern city and the seaports to the south, except for an occasional cluster of hills, there lay a vast forest, undergrown with almost impenetrable thickets and laced with hidden pools and swamps. Well into the Spanish era, when half-wild cattle and horses found hiding places in this jungle of sycamores, willows, alders, wild grape vines and bramble bushes, only a few trails penetrated it and these were made hazardous by prowling grizzly bears.

Willows helped to secure the land, but sometimes when they were planted in rows to mark a boundary they diverted an accumulation of flood waters into everdeepening ditches which soon became the jagged washes of an eroded land. Still later railroad bridges, and projects such as the ditch which was hopefully dug in Civil War times in an attempt to develop a water supply for Drum Barracks at Wilmington, acted toward the same end. Thus were formed deep cuts such as the Dominguez Wash which earlier had been but a long swale, marked by "cienegas," lakes and pools. After the floods of 1824-25 and 1832 the greater part of the marshlands north of Wilmington and Long Beach drained away through these newly defined channels. In the stagecoach era travelers wrote of crossing the plains between San Pedro and Los Angeles. The forest had disappeared.

The Gabrielino Indians knew their rivers and chose the sites of their rancherias with due regard to the whims of these streams. The prime necessities of drinking water and the daily pre-dawn bath had to be balanced by safety during the winter floods, yet mute evidence has been found to show that there were times when the only recourse they had was to their deepest magic. It has been reported that a cluster of their potent "charmstones" was once found at a point which suggested its use to help ward off an inundation. Mark Raymond Harrington was told by an old Shoshone in the desert that the Indians of the San Joaquin Valley used these stones for that purpose.

There are certain places in Los Angeles county where history, prehistory and the present meet so pointedly that it requires but little imagination to see them passing like a pageant before the inner eye. Such a spot is to be found on a certain safe and beautiful knoll which once overlooked the ancient forest and the old San Gabriel River. To reach it one drives north from San Antonio Drive in Long Beach on a road which passes the Virginia Country Club. After only a quarter of a mile there appears the Casa del Rancho Los Cerritos (the House of the Ranch of the Little Hills). At present writing this is open to the public on the afternoons of each Friday, Saturday and Sunday by courtesy of the City of Long Beach, which recently acquired the property. Here, almost at first glance, the pervasive spirit of the more leisurely tempo of old California takes possession of the visitor.

History began for this rancho in 1784 when the huge grant of which it was only a portion was made to Manuel Nieto. The adobe casa was built in 1844 by John Temple, who acquired Los Cerritos from the granddaughter, Manuela Nieto de Cota. Don Juan, as he was called, married in Santa Barbara Rafaela Cota, a cousin of Manuela's husband, and Yankee though he was entered into the life of a ranchero, dispensing hospitality in the open-handed manner of the Californian of his day. The historic drought which brought disaster to the owners of the great cattle ranches, so soon after the brief period of their greatest prosperity, caused Temple to sell Los Cerritos in 1866 to Flint, Bixby and Company, and it was from a later member of the Bixby family that Long Beach purchased the famous and beautiful Casa on this lovely eminence. The planting on the knoll and the view out over the greens of the golf course to the Palos Verdes hills on the western horizon make interesting substitutes for the vanished forest and San Gabriel River of the olden time.

Prehistory is another matter. In acquiring the famous adobe Long Beach has also come into possession of the place where perhaps once stood the Gabrielino village of *Tibahangna*, listed on the Baptismal Register as *"Tibajabit."* When John Temple built his gracious hacienda Indians helped make the adobe brick and to raise the hand-hewn redwood beams. Indians, as a matter of course, quietly performed most of the labor on which the life of the period was based, that life pictured in fiction and history as one of romantic leisure.

When the Casa del Rancho Los Cerritos was remodeled in 1930 to become a comfortable, modern residence for Llewellyn Bixby some articles were found which had belonged to earlier residents. These are displayed in a case in the room facing the patio where they were found, some rusted metal objects from the Spanish period, Gabrielino specimens such as an odd mortar and a few of the flat stone discs they rounded so precisely to use in their games. Fashioned by still earlier residents, of whom almost nothing is known, were the round stones with fluted edges, for all the world like thick, petrified sugar cookies. The use made of these "cogstones" remains a tantalizing mystery which continues to baffle the most experienced archeologist. A larger concentration of Gabrielino material was found about a half mile south of the Casa. Only thorough excavation could determine the exact site of the historic rancheria.

When given the name of "Tibahag-na" from Reid's list, J. P. Harrington's informant responded with the phrase, "de ay de la casa," which in his Shoshonean Spanish could have meant "over there from the house." He went on to say that *"Kivahangna* meant 'in the old houses'." Somewhere near the adobe casa. then, had been the rancheria, the root name of which had reached Spanish ears as *Tibaha*, although to an Indian it had been related to something from his own deep past. Had the band which settled here found habitations of earlier inhabitants, of their own tribe or of vanished predecessors? And why had not their word for house, *kiy*, come to mind? It may be stretching a thin thread to refer to the modern Hopi's name for his underground ceremonial chamber, *kiva*, in such a connection, but we do know that both languages are Shoshonean, and that *kiva* seems to have been derived from the ancient pithouses of the earliest Pueblo folk, with whom the coastal Indians had been in contact in some earlier millennium. However speculative these matters are, and must remain, we do know that through this old Gabrielino's wavering memory we are looking back into prehistory as through slowly closing doors.

Rancho Los Cerritos was only a portion of the vast acreage which was granted to José Manuel Nieto in 1784. The informal, verbal permit of Governor Fages to this soldier was confirmed to his heirs in five separate ranchos in 1834 by Governor Figueroa. Since then the original 145,000-acre tract has been cut into ever smaller and more numerous holdings. First came the large and small farms and scattered townsites, until today we find that subdivision after subdivision has created a region where more than a dozen communities, large and small, support well over 600,000 inhabitants.

In Indian times this land was dotted with many a rancheria which later gave its quota of converts to the Missions, or of servants and vaqueros to the rancheros and the other "Gente de Razon," which was the title used to distinguish the Spanish settlers from the natives, who were thought to be without reason. Today the average person would find it almost as difficult to trace the boundary of one of the old ranchos as it is to locate the site of one of the vanished Indian settlements.

Father Boscana described the place of origin of the San Juan Capistrano Indians as a village called "Sejat, distant northeast from the mission seven or eight leagues and in a valley now known by the name of 'el Rancho de los Nietos'." All that can ever be done to ascertain the location of this ancient site was accomplished in the research of John P. Harrington and outlined in great detail by him in the annotations for the

Alfred Robinson translation of Fr. Boscana's "Chinig-chinich."

Suva, or *Sehat,* Harrington discovered, was a root name meaning "wild, burrowing bee." The habits of this bee indicated the probable location to have been above a soft, earthen riverbank. The search was narrowed to five likely sites, and a few others possible but less probable. Two of these lay close to the center of the present town of Los Nietos. A great deal of Indian material has been found at a third, which Harrington described as being near the crossing of the Southern Pacific and Santa Fe Railways near Los Nietos.

Supposing that *Sehat* might have been a very early name, superseded by a later one, another possibility might have been the historic village which was on Reid's list as *"Nakaug-na,"* and placed at "Carpenter's Farm." Lemuel Carpenter was one of those North Americans who found happiness and a mild prosperity in Mexican California, only to have a tragic reversal of fortune when his own countrymen occupied the land. Soon after his arrival in 1833 he set up a soap factory, the "Jaboneria," on the west side of the present Rio Hondo, just a little south of Telegraph Road. This was on or near the site of still another of the "lodges" on Reid's list, *Chokishngna.*

Carpenter purchased the land on which stood the original adobe of Manuel Nieto, and his widow and children were using the old building as their home when it was swept away in the flood of 1867. *Naka-ungna,* therefore, lies somewhere in the middle of the channel of the "new" San Gabriel River, and if it could be proved that this was actually *Sehat* we would know the fate of that legendary village.

The fifth of these possible locations was on a knoll above the San Gabriel not far downstream from the adobe home of Don Pio Pico, the last of the governors of California in the Mexican period. Portions of this building are still standing. The village there was occupied in Spanish times, when it was called simply "La Rancheria," a specific use of the general term for any Indian settlement. A clue which might point to a pos-

sible Gabrielino name for this place is to be found in
a reference in a history of Los Angeles county, written
by three important early residents, telling of the battle
fought between the forces under General Flores and the
Americans on January 8th, 1847, at "Pico Crossing, by
the Californians always named Corunga." This is a
typical Spanish form of a typical native place-name,
yet we do not find it elsewhere. It is, however, quite
like a locative which could have been based on the
name of the woman chief, *Coronne*, who led the migrants south to become the Juaneños. The baptismal
records of San Juan Capistrano list numerous individuals who inherited forms of this clan name.

Rancho Los Alamitos, now with Los Cerritos practically synonomous with the present City of Long Beach,
was also on Nieto land. The heart of it, the Bixby
Ranch, still belongs to the descendants of early owners,
and near the ranch house, two miles inland from Alamitos Bay, once stood the great village of *Puvungna*,
the birthplace of *Chungichnish* and the place where he
revealed himself as lawgiver and god. Not far to the
northwest of this point, on a development known as
Los Altos, archeology has revealed two important sites,
but none of the traditional names can be assigned to
either of them with any certainty.

A root-name recorded for a settlement which is mentioned by Kroeber, but not found on Reid's list, is *Ahau*,
for which the locative would be *Ahaungna*. This is located by Swanton as having been on the Los Angeles
River north of Long Beach. Considering the growth of
this city northward from the sea it is quite possible that
the fairly extensive site in the vicinity of Twentieth
Street and Henderson may be the place indicated. The
stream that passed near this point in Indian times was
the old San Gabriel. It may also not be too far-fetched
to relate this name to the *Aguai* of the Baptismal Register of San Juan Capistrano, since it is known that
Gabrielinos were included among the converts of that
Mission and that *Puvungna* itself appears on the Register there. Long Beach abounds with evidences of its
ancient inhabitants whose settlements might account,

if it were possible now to learn their names, for many a "lost" entry on the Mission registers.

The coast and seaward canyons of Orange county are also thickly dotted with archeological sites. Though now largely covered over with highways and buildings, the very fact that these once existed as living communities brings to mind a picture of this shore where a contented people lived without marring the land, and with slowly evolving techniques which made increasing use of the offerings of the sea and of the brown hills that rose so sharply from the curving beaches.

A systematic excavation of one site just north of Aliso Creek, made in 1939-40, revealed a continuous occupation beginning probably about 2,000 years ago. At first the people subsisted on shell fish and the foods which they could gather in the hills. Only the upper layers of the midden contained the bones of small animals and fish, revealing a primitive hunting culture. The development here stopped short of the period immediately preceding the Spanish occupation, perhaps because of the drying up of a spring which might have forced the villagers to seek a new location. Villages which were occupied up to the advent of the Spanish or later left accumulations of bone and shell many times as extensive as were found here.

One interesting fact about this site was the discovery that the kitchen-midden continues at the same level on tiny Goff's Island, opposite the headland, showing that when this village was occupied the two were one. Here, in addition to two types of human interments, the excavators found a number of dog burials.

That other settlements along this coast persisted into Spanish times is shown by the presence of fragments of post-Mission pottery. On a recent map of archeological sites in Orange county about 65 coastal sites are shown, some of them pre-Gabrielino. At least one existed high in the hills near the Santiago Reservoir, while two important inland settlements were found at Stanton and Westminster. The latter revealed a burial ground as extensive as that excavated at Los Altos.

None of the sites along the Pacific Coast Highway

from the border at Aliso Creek northward through Laguna Beach can be titled from the rosters of the traditional names, but there are four Gabrielino names
which can be assigned to settlements in Orange county.
One of them appears on Alexander Taylor's map of
the "tribes" made in 1846. This was *Pasbengna*, on the
Santa Ana River, approximately on the spot where the
modern city of Santa Ana had its own beginnings.

Kroeber lists the root-names of *Moyo* and *Lupuk*, and
undoubtedly these equate with sites at Bolsa Chica and
Corona del Mar, respectively, since they are described
as having been located at the mouth of the Santa Ana
River and on the coast south of that point. *Hutukngna*
appears on several lists, and on the Baptismal Register
of San Gabriel. This lay on the north bank of the Santa
Ana River, a little downstream from the mouth of Santa Ana Canyon where the Bernardo Yorba adobe house
was built, itself now but a memory. The meaning of
Hutuk was "night." By way of explanation an old Gabrielino added, "For in the beginning of the world, they
went no more into the night."

When Cabrillo sailed along the Gabrielino mainland
in October of 1542, after making a landing on Santa
Catalina Island, the "numerous fires" to be seen there
prompted the giving of a title, the "Bay of Smokes."
Opinion has so differed as to whether this bay was
Santa Monica or San Pedro that one is forced to choose
between authorities. For this writer the decisions of
Bancroft and Wagner in favor of San Pedro Bay seem
the more acceptable.

In 1602 Vizcaino, beating up the coast against the
prevailing northwest wind and unable to find shelter in
San Pedro Bay, crossed to Santa Catalina Island. He,
too, saw many fires, both on the mainland and the island, which he concluded were "signals for the ships to
enter." Knowing that Indians do not make spectacular
blazes during ordinary domestic activities, one might
surmise that these were indeed signal fires, and this is
lent credence by discoveries of David Banks Rogers,
made while excavating in Santa Barbara County. He
found large beds of pure ashes which he conjectured to

be the residue from fires used as beacons to guide the fishermen or call them in from the sea. One recalls in this connection the familiar phrase, "Pillars of fire by night and of cloud by day." Another theory which has been broached, that these were brush fires set to aid in a community rabbit drive, fails in several respects to accord with known customs of the people, and does not take into consideration the mat of cactus on the headland and the swamps and forests of the lowlands.

Although Cabrillo anchored in a large "ensenada," identified by both Bancroft and Wagner as Santa Monica Bay, at no other point did he or Vizcaino touch on Gabrielino soil. The great ships passed from view and in the two centuries which elapsed between Cabrillo's voyage and the Portola expedition few other alien seafarers came within sight of this coast.

On San Pedro Bay lay one of those rare clusters of villages which are known to have owed allegiance to a single chief. The "ruling place," from which "he used to send out," was *Xuxungna*, which lay somewhere on the shore below another rancheria, *Tsauvingna*, the latter situated about where the town of San Pedro later took root. The meaning of *Xuxu* is not known, but it would be an interesting coincidence if we could see a connection between *Tsauvingna* and the Gabrielino word for fire, *tsauvut*, since this village lay in a central place on the "Bay of Smokes."

Probably the largest of all the villages of the San Pedro group was *Suangna*, and it is the only one of them listed by Reid. As he gives the location of it in the Spanish form, "Suanga," we may conclude that in 1852 this was still occupied by Indians and was a recognizable place name in that form, as Cucamonga and Topanga continue to be. It is surprising that today this village is described as having existed anywhere from the eastern part of Long Beach to San Pedro. Old residents of the harbor area recall a tradition that it was at Wilmington and this seems to tally well with the description of W. W. Robinson, who places it "overlooking in the inner bay at San Pedro," and of J. P. Harrington's informant, who said it was "on a plain, near a cienega, just east of San Pedro." *Sua* denoted the Gabrielino word for rush, *swar* or *masavit*, making this the "Place of the Rushes." Even today, if one goes "exploring" back of the harbor by the old Machado Lake, now called the Bixby Slough, one finds "cienegas" and pools fringed with the rushes for which we have borrowed the Spanish word "tules," and with a judicious closing of the eyes to various factories and highways it is not too difficult to envision the setting of *Suangna*.

It requires more of a feat of the imagination to reclothe the little hills which still stand at the entrance to San Pedro, above the intersection of Pacific Coast Boulevard and Gaffey Street, with the clusters of wickiups which once topped them. One of these was *Munikangna*, "the Place of the Small-Large Hill." The name of the other was forgotten long ago, although archeology confirms the existence of both. How astonished those old villagers would be if they could return to see the present views from their erstwhile homes: the gasoline storage tanks, railways, concrete highways and steel-hulled freighters. Or to hear the sounds which nowadays drown out the cries of the sea birds: the roar of traffic, the mournful buoys and the strident blasts from ships moving in the harbor.

The traditional names continue: *Masaungna*, a second "Place of the Rushes," and *Kinki*, also recorded as *Kinkipar* and *Kingkingna*. A village on the island of San Clemente also bore the name *Kinkipar*, and since *par* meant "water" and *Kingna*, "in the house," there is a possibility that one might translate this as "Houses by the Water." Between this village and one which also repeated an island name, *Harasgnar*, was a place which had an "old, old name," *Ataviangna*. A great cemetery had existed in the neighborhood of this important town. For what it is worth, the Gabrielino word for "big" was *ato-aviat*.

Wa-atngna, which duplicates the name of a rancheria in the San Bernardino area, was "a mile and half west of Las Salinas," near a large sycamore and a church under which were many Indian burials, according to the

Indian informants of J. P. Harrington early in our own century. The reference may have been to the salt works which were an early business enterprise at the Long Beach end of the inner bay, and which are remembered to have suffered severe damage from the various floods. There were two churches not far apart in Wilmington before the turn of the century, each large enough to impress an Indian, a fact which may suffice to locate this old village closer to the present harbor than the better remembered *Suangna*.

There were islands in San Pedro Bay in Indian times, but they are now so covered over with the harbor installations that their outlines are obscured or obliterated; and tiny Deadman's Island, which was once the sea anchor of the first breakwater, has been entirely removed. Terminal Island might not have been a friendly spot, as its early name, "Rattlesnake," implies. It is said to have been land's end for numberless reptiles, swept down from the mountains by winter storms. The pleasant dunes of Mormon Island and of Boschke's, if not the homes of Gabrielinos, must at least have made good fishing camps.

Down between the present Sepulveda and Lomita Boulevards, and then between Vermont and Figueroa, ran the long swale which the Spanish called the Cañada de Palos Verdes. This long chain of pools and swamps sometimes overflowed to enlarge Machado Lake, and the whole region all the way to the sea was vibrant with water birds. One learns, as interest in the land grows, to detect locations which an Indian would have found ideal—for instance, an eminence overlooking low ground which once held ample water for a bathing place. Archeology has in many cases confirmed such a guess. Surveys have revealed sites that may have overlooked old lakes near Compton and Gardena, and many another smaller pool, ringed perhaps with rushes and cattails and lush with watercress.

To the west of the Cañada de Palos Verdes rose the hills which continue to bear this name. Here was a vast tract of land which was inherited by the widow and children of José Dolores Sepúlveda, who was killed by Indians at La Purísima Mission during their rebellion in 1824. Throughout the Spanish and Mexican periods, and on into American times, the Sepúlvedas considered the coastal lands of their holdings to be worthless, and from the standpoint of the cattleman there is some truth in that notion. Early in the 20th Century, however, the mineral springs of White's Point were rediscovered and the carriages of the fashionable began to brave the long drive across the hills from San Pedro. No one recalled the name of the populous Indian village which had once occupied that scenic spot, but many a mortar and pestle, arrow point and stone knife went back to town with the vacationers. The "relics" found at all the habitable coves and points along that once neglected shore line were scattered and lost these many years ago, although many representative examples exist in the museums of Southern California and elsewhere.

To the amateur a collection of mortars and pestles and other stone implements, such as might be found in any of the sites, seems lacking in variety. The professional archeologist in this area, handicapped by the scarcity of stratified "digs," where cumulative levels tell their own stories of the passage of time, and handicapped also by the leaching rainfall throughout the years, can still deduce a good deal about the chronology represented by these objects.

The method of archeology used is statistical, a "mathematically objective analysis of artifact tabulations." Dr. George W. Brainerd wrote, in describing this method, that "Charles Rozaire has been able to produce an ordering of some twenty-six sites in the Los Angeles area which shows a logical pattern of change in artifact use through time. It is fixed in early-late direction by the ethnologically known late traits and European trade objects."

Malaga Cove, immediately south of Redondo Beach, was partially excavated by the Southwest Museum in 1936. This was one of the rare sites in the region in which distinct levels revealed successive occupations by quite differing peoples. David Banks Rogers, whose work in Santa Barbara county resulted in a classification of the series of cultures found there as those of the Oak Grove People, the Hunting People, and finally the Canaliño culture, found the deepest strata at Malaga Cove to represent the oldest he had ever observed. In the top layer were found European trade beads.

While the Southwest Museum published a report of the excavation, much remained to be done—a work postponed by lack of funds and the intervention of World War II. So it happened that 1955 found bulldozers at work on the upper level, biting deep into the lower ones to make the streets and drains of a modern subdivision on this magnificent site. The new owners may be surprised if the preparations for their gardens bring to view not only the broken shells and fish bones of a late Gabrielino kitchen-midden, but flakes cast off in the manufacture of ancient choppers and perhaps even bits of almost fossilized material from that deepest layer of the ancient occupation, long covered by the dunes.

Mr. Edwin Walker, who supervised the excavation here for the Southwest Museum and prepared the published report, assigned to Malaga Cove the name *"Chowig-na,"* as listed by Hugo Reid, the location being given as "Palos Verdes." In the light of the attitude of the early owners toward their coastal borders it seems more probable that this settlement was one of the many whose names have been lost. Swanton places *Chowi* in "the hills above San Pedro," and this location probably coincides with one of the known archeological sites in the region of the present reservoir, a likely spot for important villages.

Kroeber lists *Unau* as a variant for *Chowi*, while John Peabody Harrington's informants gave *Navngna* and *Unavangna* as variants, with *Chowingna* as an apparently separate name. The meaning of the former was based on the Gabrielino root, *navat*, cactus. "There used to be lots of tunas at San Pedro," said an old Gabrielino. The prevalence of this type of cactus is vividly recalled even now by some whose memories go back to childhood hours spent gathering the fruit, with many a painful scratch to pay for the harvest. If one drives down from Rolling Hills, past the reservoir and thence west to White's Point, patches of native cacti are still to be seen, looking like huddled fugitives from the farmer's plow and the subdivider's bulldozer.

One more village on the coast was *Tovemungna*, which J. P. Harrington equated with the *Tobimobit* of the San Gabriel Baptismal Register. It was named, said his informant, for a great rock, *Tovemur*, which had "placed itself at the very point of the San Pedro Hill." Such a formation exists near Point Vicente. Some years ago steatite objects were found in a cave in this vicinity.

The area from Lunada Bay down to Point Vicente and Long Point was heavily populated. Rifled by "relic" hunters and now rapidly being overlaid with construction, it still yields evidence to archeologists. Dr. William J. Wallace, of the University of Southern California, has conducted a survey of sites along this coast. He has found both early and late sites near Resort Point, as well as a second late site in the area of Malaga Cove.

The salt pools of Redondo, formed by nature at the land head of a great undersea canyon and called by the Spanish "Las Salinas," marked the terminus of an old trail from the inland settlements. The dry remnants of the pool lie on the grounds of the Southern California Edison plant. At this point stood a village remembered by variants of a name based on a root meaning salt, *engnor*. Excavations made by Wallace on the grounds of the plant and on adjacent land confirm the location of this village. Trade beads found in the upper levels show occupancy in historic times.

Down in Juaneño country a rancheria called *Engne* derived its name from a plant with a salty exudation which was used to flavor mush made from "chia" seeds, but *Engva* or *Engnovangna* at Redondo took its title from the mineral sodium chloride itself. The Gabrielinos were among the Indians who used salt in this form, although Hugo Reid was told that too much of it in a person's diet would turn his hair gray.

W. W. Robinson wrote in 1939, "On the old maps the cliffs of Ballona's easterly boundary are labelled 'Gaucho,' sometimes 'Huacho,' an Indian term meaning high place according to Cristobal Machado of Culver City, whose memory of Ballona Valley goes back to Indian Days." Machado recalled an Indian rancheria below the present Loyola University and another near the site of his old family home in the vicinity of the present Overland and Jefferson Boulevards. These were the late survivors of settlements of which archeological surveys have found the remains of at least 14 along Ballona Creek and the bluffs to the south. One of these could perhaps have been the traditional village, *Sa-an*, root-name of a village placed by Swanton "on the coast south of Santa Monica."

It was in this general region that the heavily fossilized bones of "Los Angeles Man" were found 12 to 13 feet below the surface. In the same stratum occurred bones of the mammoth, the fluorine content of which matched that found in the human bones, indicating their contemporaneous existence. Bones found in Angeles Mesa, certain of the human remains recovered from the Brea Pits, and material from Level One of Malaga Cove form additional evidence of occupation by man long before the arrival of the Gabrielinos.

Sa-an does not seem to appear on the Baptismal Registers, but the entry *"Coronababit"* may refer to the *Kuruvungna* at Santa Monica or to a village of a similar name near Saboba Hot Springs. Both of these meant "Place where we are in the sun." This brings to mind the rather scornful comments of Father Boscana to the effect that the greatest luxury of his Indian charges was to lie basking in the sun. Except for rainy winter days, or in the damp, rolling fogs which reduced life to a dumb misery, these forerunners of our modern sunbathers found theirs the most pleasant of worlds.

North of Santa Monica there were Gabrielino villages near the mouths of Santa Ynez and Topanga Canyons. At the latter place, it was recalled, there had been a great cemetery with whale bones erected over the graves, a practice typically Canaliño. As an immense amount of commercial "pot-hunting" went on in all the coastal area, practically all evidence of *Topangna* disappeared long ago. Farther up the canyon sites of more ancient inhabitants have been excavated and reports have been published.

This completes the roster of the known names of coastal villages. We may be sure that there were many others on the high places overlooking pools and streams, such as those which the Spanish called La Centinela and the Rodeo de las Aguas, "the Gathering of the Waters." The farther inland they lay, the less was the life attuned to the moods of the sea.

The Gabrielinos of the coast led hardy lives as traders, seafarers, fishermen. Day after day, as they looked out over the restless ocean, they grew to know *kjot*, the whale, *wajnuk*, the seal, *wesara*, the sea gull. To them the *torovim*, the porpoise, was an intelligent being, created for the definite mission of guarding *Tovangnar*, the Whole World. The "porpoises were like men, not like women," and wore the feather head-dresses. One of the great Gabrielino ceremonies, danced in the full regalia of eagle-feather skirt and head-tuft, was called the *torovim*. It was held in honor of the faithful guardians, who now and again could be seen far out to sea, carrying out their eternal circuit in order to ensure the safety and well-being of the Gabrielino world.

The Islands

Spanish Exploration by Sea

Visible from the mainland lay the islands to which the Spanish were to affix the melodious names of Santa Catalina and San Clemente, and beyond was small San Nicolas. The Gabrielinos had a descriptive phrase for them. *"Wexaj momte asunga wow,"* they said: "Mountain ranges that are in the sea."

The language spoken on all these islands and perhaps on tiny Santa Barbara Island as well, was Shoshonean. The dialect of the most dominant of the group, Santa Catalina, was Gabrielino, and it is probable that this was also true of San Clemente. The speech of the inhabitants of the Channel Islands off the Ventura-Santa Barbara coast was Chumash, but the material culture of the entire group at the time of the advent of the Spanish, is classified under the term "Canaliño."

True to form, the mainland Gabrielinos found something uncanny, even sinister, in the isolation granted their tribesmen by the rough waters of the channel. Although brisk trading went on between them, and the mainland had learned from the religious genius of the men of Santa Catalina many of the elements of their vigorous *Chungichnish* cult, it was whispered that while the shamans of the mainland might kill their enemies with poison, those of the islands were fierce wizards who used wolves to carry out their lethal designs.

The Luiseño Indians had a similar respect for the men of Santa Catalina. One of the informants of Helen H. Roberts told her that these islanders "knew better" than the folk of the mainland, that they could "prophesy truly." It was believed that they lived two or three hundred years and were so strong they could bend trees. These trees were like gods, it was said. They were frequently named in songs by a clan from Santa Catalina which had migrated to the mainland, whereupon all that they "called for would come true."

The Spanish, when the turn of history brought them to Santa Catalina in October, 1542, saw nothing at all to fear in these fishermen and artisans in basketry and stone. As Juan Rodriguez Cabrillo's ships came to anchor the natives took up their bows, while their women and children fled to hide in the chaparral, but the explorers managed to convey by signs convincing proof of their peaceful intent. Soon the Spaniards went ashore, amid what seems to have been a feeling of friendliness and mutual trust.

An even more cordial reception was accorded the Vizcaino party in 1602, which was beckoned to shore by signal fires. The author of the general diary of that expedition wrote: "We anchored, and the admiral, Ensign Alarcon, Father Fray Antonio, and Captain Peguero, with some soldiers, went ashore. Many Indians were on the beach, and the women treated us to roasted sardines and a small fruit like sweet potatoes."

Thus, almost casually, are reported the earliest meetings of these Indians, so long established on their peaceful shores, with the restless Europeans who were wel-

One of the plank canoes in which the Gabrielinos traveled from village to village on the mainland and islands.

comed with shouts and "great rejoicings." Many elements of drama are present in these events, and not the least of them lies in the extraordinary courage of the explorers in their small, poor ships, with simple navigation equipment and inadequate stores of food and water. A description of the symptoms of scurvy, as penned by Father Juan de Torquemada from the records of the Vizcaino expedition removes from these oft-told events any tinge of mere romantic adventure.

Although Vizcaino went on to explore Monterey Bay he saw little more of the coast than had Cabrillo, 60 years earlier, or Cermeno during the intervening years. He visualized the use of this bay as a port of call for the treasure ship, the Manila Galleon, which annually reached a point almost, if not quite, as far north as Cape Mendocino before turning to sail before the northwest wind to a haven in Mexico, sometimes running a gauntlet of freebooters on the way. Critics point out that these ships stood out to sea a hundred or more miles at the most northerly point, and that San Diego would have made a much better port and one far closer to sources of supply and defense.

However Vizcaino's motives and accomplishments may be evaluated, he was an intrepid explorer, and he and his chroniclers left a mass of reports that became the sources for historians, from Father Torquemada and Venegas down to those of today. The original narratives and "representations" were intended to influence His Majesty, Philip III of Spain, to order a second expedition. During a long delay, while this was under consideration, Vizcaino died. All his ambitious plans for the settling of California and the conversion to Christianity of the thousands of Indian inhabitants, for whose souls, "going to destruction," he apparently felt a genuine concern, went into the dusty archives of Spain and Mexico.

The importance, to our study, of these expeditions lies in these diaries and narrations. Venegas quoted from them in his descriptions of the women of Santa Catalina as handsome, with lovely eyes and features, and of the children as fair, affable and usually smiling. The writer of the Vizcaino diary reported that the faces of the women showed them to be modest. All seemed to agree, however, that the men added a talent for thievery to their general cleverness and first-rate intelligence.

Soon after their landing, probably in Avalon bay, the ships moved to an anchorage in the Port of Catalina, on the seaward side of the isthmus. Here, the diarist wrote, "The general went inland to see the opposite coast. He found on the way a level prairie, very well cleared, where the Indians were assembled to worship an idol which was there. It resembled a demon, having two horns, no head, a dog at its feet, and many children painted all around it. The Indians told the General not to go near it but he approached it and saw the whole thing, and made a cross, and placed the name of Jesus on the head of the demon, telling the Indians that that was good, and of heaven, but that the idol was the devil. At this the Indians marvelled, and they will readily renounce it and receive our Holy Faith, for apparently they have good intellects and are friendly and desirous of our friendship."

Other records called this clearing a "patio" and described the "temple" as a large circle, surrounded by feathers from birds which the Indians had sacrificed. At one side of the figure painted "like a demon" was an image of the sun, at the other one of the moon. While the party was visiting the spot two ravens flew from the enclosure to some rocks. The soldiers killed them with their arquebuses, which threw the Indians into the wildest lamentation. The devil, explained the writer, talked to the natives through the ravens.

The skill of the islanders as fishermen was described by such adjectives as graceful, easy and pleasant. Sea lions and large fish were caught with bone harpoons which were fastened to the ends of thin willow rods tied with long cords. So impressed were the Spanish by the plank boats that they credited them as being large enough to carry 20 men, adding that they were often managed by only two, with a boy along "to bail out the water which flows in."

Basketry water bottle.

We read: "The general gave them beads and they gave him prickly pears and a grain like the *gofio* of the Canary Islands, in some wicker baskets very well made, and water in vessels resembling flasks which were like rattan inside and very thickly varnished outside. They had acorns and some very heavy skins, apparently of bears, with heavy fur, which they used for blankets." The diarist noted the trading prowess of the Indians who produced, in exchange for old clothes, "skins, nets, thread, and very well-twisted ropes, these in great quantities and resembling linen."

Through these records we can clearly visualize these Indians in their prehistoric state as members of a stable, primitive society, clean in body, healthy, skillful artisans, boatmen and fishermen of grace and skill, and also deeply religious in their own tradition. Where in these earliest portraits of the island Gabrielinos do we find the mythical "digger Indians," the lazy degenerates, the filthy and loutish folk which the later tradition set up as typical of the natives of this tribe?

One of the authors whose first-hand reports of the

expedition of Sebastian Vizcaino afforded material for the later historians was Fray Antonio de la Ascension. In 1620 one of his reports was forwarded to the Viceroy of Mexico. This was accompanied by a "Memorial" by one Francisco de Arellano which read as follows:

"A Brief Report in which is given the Information of the Discovery which was made in New Spain, in the South Sea, from the Port of Acapulco to a Point beyond Cape Mendocino; containing an Account of the Riches, the Temperate Climate, and the Advantages of the Realm of the Californias, and setting forth how his Majesty will be able at little cost to pacify it and incorporate it into His Royal Crown and cause the Holy Gospel to be preached in it. By Father Fray Antonio de la Ascension, a Religious of the Discalced Order of Carmelites, who took part in it and as Cosmographer made a map of it."

It is possible that Fray Ascension pictured himself in the role which the Franciscan Father Serra was to play in reality many years later, for he left not only a glowing description of the country but detailed suggestions for organizing the occupation. The guard, he recommended, should contain no less than 200 "good and honorable men," who must be expert and experienced seamen and soldiers as well. Two captains would be needed, "good Christians and God-fearing men." These were to "hold themselves in strict obedience and subjection to the religious who are of their company." Without the priests' order, counsel and advice war might not be made "or the heathen Indians be otherwise molested."

Another of the stipulations of Fray Ascension was that no woman should embark on the expedition, "in order to avoid offenses to God and dissensions between one another." Throughout his report he stresses that only love and affection must be shown the Indians. Their possessions must be respected, so that they will learn to obey the Spaniards "without opposition or repugnance" and find good reason to be grateful and

to give willing assistance. He does, however, advise a
watch tower and a continuous sentinel. These provisions make interesting reading when compared to the
actual plans for the founding of the Franciscan Missions, and to the events which took place in actuality.

For a century and a half after this "Memorial" was
sent to the Viceroy the Indians could dance in their
tobet feathers undisturbed. But when, at last, Spain
took over this land the teeming population began at
once to diminish. Diseases for which the native constitution had set up no resistance took a fearful toll. However, when the end came for these peaceful islanders
Spain and her successor, Mexico, were only indirectly
involved. The rich furs, which the diarist of the Vizcaino party thought might be bear robes but which
were in reality the skins of sea otters, drew hunters of
every adventurous race of man able to reach these
islands in the sailing ships of the time.

The islanders were no match for the fierce Aleuts
who came as hunters in the crews of Russian ships, or
for Kanakas brought in by American sailing vessels.
Ruthless and violent warfare very nearly exterminated
both the sea otter and the Indians. The time came when
the hunting was no longer profitable, but before that
the settlements in the coves and inlets had dwindled
to the point where it became the better part of mercy
to remove the survivors to the mainland. Refugees from

Miniature canoe carved of steatite by California Indians.

San Clemente were assigned to Mission San Luis Rey, which may possibly account for a report that the ancient dialect of that island had been Luiseño. Although San Gabriel is said to have been the destination of those from Santa Catalina, it is on a list compiled from the Baptismal Register of San Fernando that we find the name *"Pipimas,"* and in parentheses following, "Islas."

San Nicolas suffered most cruelly. It has been said that Kodiaks, left on the island to hunt, massacred the men and appropriated their families. Some 20 survivors were rounded up and taken to San Pedro in 1835. Amid the confusion of the evacuation, however, one woman, discovering that her child had been left behind, leaped from the rescue boat and swam back to shore. Because of the high gales and heavy surf the boat had to leave without her. Its captain intended to return later for the woman, but after delivering his Indian charges safely to the mainland his craft was lost in a subsequent storm.

For years this "female Robinson Crusoe" was forgotten—until California passed into American hands and occasional fishermen reported seeing someone wandering over the island plateau. In 1850 a search of the island failed to reveal a single human being but the party returned to Santa Barbara with the news of a resurgence among the sea otters and the black seals. New hunts, by local crews, were organized and on the third of these, in 1853, traces of human occupancy were discovered which led to the finding of the "lost woman of San Nicolas." She was dressed in a tunic of satiny green cormorant feathers and her first act was to prepare a meal for her guests from her small store of roasted roots.

This intrepid woman lived but a few months after her rescue. No trace of a single member of the party which had preceded her to the mainland 18 years earlier could be found, and no Indian who was brought to see her, not even a few natives of Santa Catalina, could understand her dialect, although it seemed to be from Shoshonean stock. It has been reported that her dress and other belongings were sent to the Vatican.

This story of the "Lost Woman of San Nicolas," although not fictional, has become a legend and is told in many versions. The outline given above is based on an article printed in *Scribner's Magazine* in 1880. Emma Hardacre, the author, came to Santa Barbara in 1876 and knew several of the people who took part in the rescue. She made every effort to produce a factual report.

Mrs. Hardacre also met and talked to M. Leon de Cessac, whom she described as "a gentleman engaged in collecting archeological specimens for the French Government." The activities of this French scientist account for the amazing knowledge some Europeans have of our local Channel Island culture. M. de Cessac also discovered in Santa Barbara, and managed to secure for France, a second original manuscript of Father Boscana's *"Chinigchinich."*

This may be the one which was translated by John Peabody Harrington, which differs in some details from the manuscript translated by the early pioneer resident, Alfred Robinson.

The island of San Nicolas, which for years boasted a population of one Basque sheepherder, with his dogs, sheep, and the howling wind for company, now belongs to the U.S. Navy and is occupied by several hundred naval and civilian personnel engaged in the work of the naval air missile testing program. The wind, the ravens, the sea elephants and sea lions are still there, as are evidences of the Indian past. Generations of collectors, some genuinely scientific in spirit, others who can only be called "pot-hunters," have removed literally tons of archeological material from the Channel Islands, even from this most distant and lonely of the group, but no one can quite obliterate the accumulations of centuries of the numerous and skillful fishermen and artisans who lived there.

Few individuals, other than the naval and civilian personnel stationed on San Nicolas and San Clemente, are enabled to view these outlying islands. Santa Catalina, on the contrary, is visited by a great number of tourists each year, and of these many join the guided bus tours into the interior. Circumscribed as these necessarily are, they do traverse mountain ridges, canyons and inlets, and afford lovely vistas of the sea. These comparatively isolated regions stimulate the imagination of one bent on reconstructing the aboriginal scene.

Throughout these tours distressing evidences of erosion cannot be ignored. These can be explained, not only by the cycle of drought which afflicts the Southwest, but by the industrious grazing and rooting of the descendants of tame animals left on the island by white voyagers. The now wild goats and boars have multiplied enormously, and to their efforts have been added those of a small herd of bison, veterans of a movie production left behind when the rest of the cast returned to the mainland.

If today Santa Catalina Island were to be restored to the ownership of the Gabrielinos of old it is doubtful that they could live at their ancient high standard. Certainly, the busy pigs and piglets of the wild boar population must have enormously reduced one great resource, the roots which flourished so well that the Spanish reported them as part of the native export trade with the mainland. Their loss undoubtedly contributes to the great areas of loose, dusty soil, waiting to be washed or blown away at the first rain or gale.

Of these roots, those that Vizcaino's men compared to the sweet potato may have been of the wild cucumber, or Big Root, which was common on the islands. The Spanish called these "jicamas" or "xicamas." The Indians exported the smaller ones, but some of them grew to be quite enormous. The men of the Cermeno expedition in 1595 ate cakes prepared from these on San Martin Island, off Lower California, and were made quite ill as they seemed to have purgative qualities dangerous to the unaccustomed. Another favorite food found on both the islands and the mainland was the roots, or rather corms, of the Brodiaea, that lovely spring flower of heavenly blue which still survives, though sparsely. The Spanish named these nut-flavored morsels "cacomites," from the Aztec *"cacomitl."*

The traveling public gains a very faint idea of the

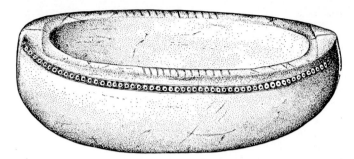

Miniature stone canoe with beaded decoration.

once flourishing Indian life on Santa Catalina. On one tour, as the bus skirts the heights above Little Harbor, "the Indian burial ground" is pointed out far below, and as the escarpment is rounded the trenches of an archeological dig made by the University of California, Los Angeles, in 1953 are viewed. These two glimpses, interesting as they are, afford but a meagre notion of the discoveries which have been made in regard to the Indians of the island.

Luckily for those who would like a more comprehensive picture of Santa Catalina as it used to be, one can turn to the writings of Charles Frederick Holder, zoologist and sportsman, founder of the famous Tuna Club. One of Holder's first impressions on his arrival there in 1886 concerned the rollicking antics and the ingrained impudence of the many ravens which were constantly stealing little chickens and turkeys from the ranch of "Chicken John," in a canyon back of Avalon. The privileged status of these birds during the centuries of Indian tenancy was soon made evident to the newcomer as he entered wholeheartedly into historical research, consulting the records of the Vizcaino party and the work of Father Boscana in order to establish a background for the fine descriptive passages he was to write.

Among the many unforgettable scenes Holder recorded were the dunes of lonely San Nicolas. They "cover and uncover the dead," he wrote. "They fill the canyons, form strange shapes which float in the air before they are carried away." He described a "mesa of pebbles which leap into the air and blow about" and "great natural stair-cases leading from mesa to beach." The Basque sheepherder was firm in the belief that the spirits were angry and made the wind blow because of the "grave-robbing" which had been carried on so extensively.

"At the west end of the island lay a great kitchen-midden about ten feet high and extending over a mile," Holder wrote. It was "made up of shells of various kinds, mostly abalones, thrown here for ages. In this area are graves of countless natives who were buried in the long ago. As each man was buried with all his possessions there is an object in grave-robbing. Scores of parties have explored here, and doubtless the region has hardly been touched on."

In addition to the familiar objects of stone found in typical Gabrielino sites, Holder mentioned seeing objects of wood, but did not describe them in detail. These would be of more than ordinary interest to the modern student, as time and the custom of cremating the dead of the inland villages has left somewhat of a gap in our knowledge of the material culture in so far as the use of wood is concerned. Holder told of one "collector" who found implements stored in "coffins" of wood. He himself saw fishing lines made of "bull kelp" still attached to the equipment, although the Spanish reported cord and rope "as fine as linen." He also saw, in a collection, a long stone club, "doubtless a token of office" as it was "an extraordinary weapon."

A custom of the island Indians was to preserve their small treasures in abalone shells cemented together with asphalt. One of these was presented to the Southwest Museum by W. H. Burnham, who purchased it from a collector, and countless visitors have found it of great interest. Displayed near it is an X-ray photograph of the contents, as this prehistoric jewel case has never been opened since it was sealed by the original owner.

Continuing with his description of San Nicolas

Holder wrote, "I found one spot years ago which must have been a battlefield similar to the one I found at San Clemente. Skeletons were piled up, skulls crushed, and bones broken; while mortars too heavy to carry off were strewn about—a perfect golgotha." San Nicolas, he recalled, had been ravaged by the Russians from Alaska.

De Cessac, during his excavations on San Nicolas, in the period of 1877 to 1879, also found many examples of the work of Northwest Indians, ample proof of the visits of the hunters of the sea otter. This French scientist held the opinion that the culture of San Nicolas was related to that of San Clemente and Santa Catalina, rather than to the islands off the coast of Santa Barbara County. He was particularly eloquent in regard to the exquisite stone work, beautifully turned mortars and pestles, and small carvings of the creatures of sea, land and air. De Cessac was fascinated, as many have been since his time, with the odd hook-shaped stone carvings which resemble conventionalized pelicans; or, as Heizer expresses it, "the scheme or embryo of the statue of a cetacean." These may have been fetiches. One can see the possibility of such a use in the small carvings of boats, some of them inlaid with decorations of shell, to bring home safely men who braved the sea in plank canoes.

Holder's account of a trip made in 1907 across San Clemente is a classic. Of one episode he wrote, "We climbed the steep hill at Howland's and were shortly on the remarkable sand-dunes; where the first view of the ancient town sites became apparent. The long billowy white sand, a menace to the island, filling the cañons, was dotted here and there with human bones and broken skulls." On the island Holder saw an entire mesa "covered with midden and broken implements." At the base of a "lava" flow a midden lay in front of a cave. He described "lava" cliffs cut by cañons, "gaping, uncanny caves" and gleaming heaps of abalones, most of these long ago exported to be resold here and elsewhere in the shape of pearl buttons and trinkets.

Steatite effigy of killer whale carved by Southern California Indians. These range in size from less than an inch to seven or eight inches in length.

Of Santa Catalina Holder wrote, as late as 1909, "When a trench is dug in any part of Avalon today, especially along the north beach, shells, implements, and ancient human bones are often found, and the black earth crops out, telling the story of one of the most interesting ancient archeological treasure-houses in America." He describes the work and "collections" of various men who excavated in the many village sites which existed at the Isthmus, at "every cañon having a beach along the north coast." Specific locations were mentioned at Catalina Harbor, Little Harbor, Johnson's Landing, Empire Landing, White's Landing and many another inlet. Signs of occupation were also found at far less accessible places, as in caves at considerable altitudes.

Holder found "the old quarry at Empire landing, with its myriads of chips and flints, just as though the workers had been driven off and forced to drop their possessions and run." Here in the chaparral were out-croppings of steatite and the clear evidences of a pre-historic stone works. It seemed that the plan of the van-ished artisans had been to "chip out a mortar with their rude implements until it resembled a ball the size of a man's head or larger, connected by a small stem. This sphere was knocked or broken off, and then hol-lowed out—doubtless by women—by a tedious process with stone implements . . ." The explorer saw "half-made mortars, others a third made, still fastened to the rock, almost perfect ones in the bush hard by, while the steatite ledge was covered in places with the scars of mortars which had been successfully removed."

Among the early excavators on the Channel Islands were Stephen Bowers, for the American Museum of Natural History and Paul Schumacher, who was com-missioned by the United States Government and sent huge collections to the Smithsonian Institution and to the Peabody Museum in the 1870s. In 1887 Dr. Hold-er and Dr. William Channing of Boston "trenched down through four or five layers of graves at the Isth-mus." The upper layers contained European objects but nothing made of metal was found in the lower strata.

Excavations have been made by contemporary scien-tists, who are aided by the methods developed by mod-ern archeology but severely handicapped by the whole-sale destruction of most of the sites by "pot-hunters" of the past. Notable among the more recent archeologists who have worked on the Channel Islands are Bruce Bryan, Malcolm Rogers, Arthur Woodward and Phil Orr. An article in the October, 1953, issue of *American Antiquity* by Clement W. Meighan and Hal Eberhart reports a reconnaissance of San Nicolas Island made by these two writers and summarizes the work of those mentioned above.

At various times between 1958 and 1960 Charles Rozaire and Bruce Bryan of the Southwest Museum have worked on San Nicolas Island, and the results have been published in short papers in *The Masterkey*, published by the museum. A richly stratified site was excavated on the southeast shore of the island which yielded numerous examples of material woven from sea grass (grass skirts, mats, etc.). Several new and unknown types of selvage were included among these fragments, some of which were found at a depth of about nine feet. Two or three metates, considered by some to have been lacking in San Nicolas culture, were also found by the Southwest Museum.

In 1959, on the same island, archeologists of the University of California, Los Angeles, found a group of very interesting burials with which many tarred baskets were closely associated. This university is at present doing work at various sites on San Nicolas, San Clemente and Anacapa Islands.

An answer to the question of whether or not these islands were occupied before the coming of the Gabrielinos seems to be given in the affirmative in the recent excavation by Meighan, the one which may be viewed by tourists on the crest of the heights above Little Harbor on Santa Catalina. Here there was evidence of an occupancy going back at least 4,000 years, which well antedates the probable arrival of the Indians of Shoshonean stock. The settlement below, in Little Harbor itself, had been so thoroughly gutted by pot-hunters that not much could be learned about it, although it was certainly Gabrielino and occupied in historic times as the U.C.L.A. party found trade beads at the site.

Meighan believed the material he found on San Nicolas to go back less than a thousand years, but Orr saw parallels there with discoveries he had made on Santa Rosa of a "Dune Dweller" culture of great antiquity. Carbon-14 tests have placed materials from Dune Dweller burials on the latter, more northern, island at about 7,000 years ago. More recently, in still older strata on Santa Rosa, Orr has found charred bones of an extinct Ice Age "dwarf" elephant that had apparently been cooked and eaten by man. These have been dated by Carbon-14 as being about 29,000 years old.

No such sensational finds have been made in the

southern group, although one cannot predict what knowledge could come from comprehensive work, backed with sufficient funds and carried on by such reputable men and institutions as have done the recent surveys and excavations.

It is impossible to apply with any degree of certainty any of the traditional Gabrielino place names to the villages which once existed on Santa Catalina, although the island itself is listed by Reid as *Pineug-na*, by Kroeber as *Pimu* and *Pipimar*, and by J. P. Harrington as *Pimu'na*, with "n" indicated as nasal, a form we have been transcribing as "ngna." *Limu*, as found in a record of an early Spanish explorer, was probably an incorrect recording of *Pimu*. The Baptismal Register, as noted above, listed *Pipimas* and the few survivors of the island were known as the *Pipimares*.

Holder did not use a single native name in his decriptions of the village sites on Santa Catalina, but in a work of fiction for juveniles, "The Adventures of Torqua," he made use of "literary license" in applying names from Reid's list—and one less fortunately chosen from Chumash sources — to the localities which his young Indian and Spanish heroes visited. Unfortunately an early pamphlet on the subject of Santa Catalina appears to have copied two of these as factual, and thus set off a chain of repetition of these place names which seem to have no other claim to authenticity.

Reid assigned the name *Kinkipar* to San Clemente Island, but Swanton calls this the name of "a village on San Clemente." As this duplicates that of a village in the San Pedro area, the meaning of which could perhaps be "Houses by the Sea," the application of the name to a village rather than to the island itself is confirmed by the small item of evidence.

An insoluble puzzle may lie in the name on Reid's list, *Harasg-na*, the only one which he gave without assigning a location. This was mentioned by J. P. Harrington's informants as being "a place near San Pedro," but also, as *Xarasngna*, quite clearly described as San Clemente Island. Gudde also mentions *Kimki harasa* as the Luiseño name for San Clemente.

So far this information appears to harmonize, but one cannot ignore the fact that *Ghalas-at*, the Chumash title for San Nicolas, as Kroeber points out, is probably the Chumash form of the Gabrielino *Harasg-na*, as recorded by Reid. The similarity is made more apparent when it is remembered that the northern tribe had no sound "r" and that "l" would be the normal substitute.

J. P. Harrington's notes give the origin of this name in the term *ijoxarin*, meaning "stony," probably in the sense of "eroded," as his informants went on to explain this in the phrase, "We are living in the island of the uncovered earth." This is certainly an apt description of San Nicolas, although San Clemente need not be excluded as a contender for the title.

An Indian of Santa Catalina would have been known as a *Pimuvit*, these old Gabrielinos agreed, but when at last there existed but a few individuals who traced their ancestry to the island they were known to the folk of the Pueblo of Los Angeles, near which they existed in a tiny settlement, not as *Pimuvitam* but as the *Pipimares*. They no longer seemed, to their almost equally diminished tribesmen of the mainland, the fierce wizards who had once fared across the rough channel waters from the mysterious stronghold of their island home. They were mild, quiet and aloof, and quite soon they disappeared entirely from the dusty streets of the Pueblo, as they had some years earlier from their beloved "mountains which are in the sea."

The Great Valleys

Spanish Exploration by Land

More than a century and a half elapsed between the voyage of Vizcaino, which had resulted in his earnest appeal for the settlement of Upper California, and the first landward approach to Monterey Bay made by the Spanish. During this long period the surge of energy which for us is typified by such figures as Columbus and Cortez seemed to have died down. The dream of treasure which had lured Coronado northward, sparked by tales of fabulous Tusayan, Cibola and Quivira, had long ago faded in the realities of the poor pueblos of Arizona and New Mexico, and the blizzard-swept plains beyond. Yet the arrival in Mexico in 1765 of the newly-appointed Visitador-General, the powerful Don José de Gálvez, the highest ranking person to

Franciscan Order arms carved by Indians.

reach that province since Cortez himself, marked the beginning of a new and successful effort of conquest and colonization.

Gálvez traveled to Lower California, where not long before the Franciscan Order had replaced that of the Jesuits, in order to reorganize the Missions there and to plan the exploration and occupation of the land to the north. San Diego was named as the meeting place of four parties, two going by sea and two by land. The military commanders appointed to lead the land expeditions were Captains Fernando Rivera y Moncada and Gaspar de Portolá. In Father Junípero Serra, whom Gálvez named President of the Missions, he had found a spirit on fire to Christianize the natives of this land which the soldiers were to conquer for the Crown of Spain.

The two "paquebotes," the "San Antonio" and the "San Carlos," reached the designated rendezvous first, on April 11 and 29, 1769, respectively. Scurvy had claimed the lives of more than a third of their total crews, the men on the "San Carlos" suffering so badly that no one was able to lower a boat after the anchor had been dropped.

The land expeditions joined them on May 14 and July 1. After a revision of the original plans the "San Antonio" returned to San Blas for new sailors and supplies. the "San Carlos" remained at anchor in the bay, and 40 men began the construction of the first rude shelters of a permanent settlement.

A reorganized land party set off to the north immediately, under the command of Don Gaspar de Portolá, even before Father Serra had dedicated the first of the Missions to San Diego de Alcalá, on July 16. The plan was to re-locate Monterey Bay and the hope was to be met there by a third ship, the "San José." With the man-power and supplies she would bring the Spaniards hoped to set up at this point a presidio and a second Mission.

Neither of these objectives materialized during the first expedition. Monterey Bay, which had become a legend of a great harbor, was passed unrecognized; the

"San José" failed to appear. Exploration continued until sickness and limited supplies turned the party back, but members of it reached the peninsula on which was one day to be built the city of San Francisco, and viewed from various points the sea and bay which they knew represented formidable barriers to farther progress northward.

The expedition returned to San Diego, reaching there on January 24, 1770, after six months and 10 days, only to find the little settlement reduced by sickness and death to half its original strength. There had been indifference and armed hostility on the part of the Indians, later called Diegueños. It seemed to Portolá that the wisest thing to do would be to return to the starting point, Velicatá, in Lower California. In this he was opposed by Fathers Serra and Crespi, and by the captain of the "San Carlos." The latter won the debate, probably because of the return of the "San Antonio" with fresh supplies and new orders. Immediately after the celebration of the Easter feast, the first observance of this day in California, Portolá set off once more. This time the land party and the "San Antonio" reached Monterey a week apart in late May. On June 3, 1770, Father Serra with Father Juan Crespi as his associate founded the second Mission, San Carlos Borromeo de Monterey, and Portolá raised the royal standard over the new presidio.

Thus the land of the Gabrielino Indians had been crossed three times in that first year of the Spanish regime. It was during the first expedition, on July 24, 1769, to be exact, that European explorers had made the first camp on their borders, on high ground overlooking a stream. Indians from a village down in the canyon had visited the newcomers. They came unarmed, bearing gifts of seeds and shells and receiving "ribbons and trifles" in return. It has been surmised from the records of the expedition that this camp was on the heights overlooking Aliso Creek, near the present town of El Toro, in Orange county.

We can see the land as it looked then through the eyes of Father Juan Crespi, whose diary of the initial exploration is probably the best known of several which were kept: the streams, the rolling hills with oaks and walnut trees spaced as in broad parks, the plains covered with the thick, soft, native grasses, as yet uncrowded by the descendants of those stowaways, the wild oats from the Mediterranean. It was a land of contrasts, of "low woods" formed of the stubborn manzanita and other slow-growing trees, of thickets of alders and sycamores by swampy lowlands, of tangles of wild grapevines, and masses of wild roses whose riotous blooms in midsummer made the soldiers homesick for Spain. "Roses of Castile" they called them, remembering suddenly the flowers of their native land which few of them would ever see again.

Father Crespi, though he was amazed by the unabashed nakedness of the men and children, was pleased with the simple natives, a few of whom repeated after him some of the phrases from his prayers and showed what he felt was reverence for the symbols of his religion. There can be little doubt that the Indians believed these bearded soldiers and the two gray-robed priests to be gods, mounted as they were on great, tame beasts. Always the natives approached timidly, holding out baskets full of their simple gifts, sometimes "howling like wolves," and on one occasion blowing puffs of smoke toward the newcomers from their ceremonial pipes of steatite.

Miguel Costansó, engineer and map-maker, a man whose creative mind left a stamp on the development of California out of proportion to his short stay, recorded in his diary the directions taken and the distances covered during each day's march, and for a large part they agree with the observations of Father Crespi. Outstanding natural features, the mountains and rivers, were given names by Father Crespi, names chosen from the Saint's days of those summer weeks. It would seem, however, that others of his countrymen had talents along this line, too, since most of his titles have been superseded.

Just before the expedition reached the first camp in Gabrielino country it had left the coast, traveling along a creek inland from the present San Juan Capistrano. Here it had passed several villages, one of which could have been on the site of the legendary *Putuidem*, the first settlement made by the migrants from *Sehat* in the Los Nietos region under the leadership of *Coronne*, their woman chief. From Aliso Creek, the first camp, they continued along the Santiago Hills to a second near some springs which Father Crespi named for San Panteleón, though the soldiers called them the Springs of Father Gomez, the second priest of the party, who had discovered this source of good water.

The next day's route followed the Santa Ana River to a pleasant spot where 52 Indians from a "populous" village offered gifts. This may have been *Hutukngna*, "Place of Night," which was also transcribed as *Jutucunga* and *Jutacabit* on Spanish records. The site of this is given by J. P. Harrington as on the north bank of the Santa Ana River, a little downstream from Santa Ana Canyon. Here the Spaniards were welcomed most cordially, with offerings of antelope and rabbit meat, and signs to show the desire of the natives to keep their guests as permanent residents. The occurrence of severe earthquakes threw the natives into demonstrations of fear and undoubtedly added to the respect the newcomers received. The Spaniards may have been able to conceal their own dismay, but the river was promptly dubbed the "Rio de Los Temblores," though the soldiers already had named it for Saint Anne.

The abundance of food on hand at this place gives a hint that a religious rite was being planned, and this was found to be in progress at a village near which the expedition camped on the following night. This may have been in lower reaches of Brea Canyon. The diarists recorded that it lay by a small pool, and that the population was swelled by the presence of the natives who had been their hosts on the previous evening. No one thought to ask the Indian name of any of the rancherias which were mentioned in the diaries, but we do have here probably the earliest mention of the local custom of ceremonial reciprocity, and it is safe to assume that the two rancherias were of different but associated clans.

The Spaniards continued across the Puente Hills, probably by way of La Habra. Had they gone a little to the east of their actual route, through Brea Canyon and down the present Brea Canyon cut-off road, they would have descended into a secluded "corner" in the northern face of the hills which was later named just that — the "Rancho Rincon de La Brea" — when it became the property of one Gil Ybarra. This was the home of an important village which was to give many a convert to the San Gabriel Mission, where it was listed as "Pomoquin," although the better known form of it was *Pimocangna*, and it was also recorded as *Pumu'kingna*. This was associated in the memory of one of J. P. Harrington's informants with the idea of sleeping outside of the house, as in the "beginning of the world," when the first people slept, naked and cold, not in houses but in the open.

Father Crespi and Costansó agreed that they traveled next day a distance of four leagues (approximately nine and a half miles) to a camp by a river which was running so briskly, and with banks so miry and lush with water cress, that they had to make a bridge of poles in order to cross it. They do not mention seeing any Indian habitations, though this was the most populous valley of them all, the one which would finally be named for San Gabriel Arcángel though at the time they honored the Archangel Michael instead.

To the north of this valley rose mountains "high and dark," with many "corrugations," and the floor of it had an "abundance of water, some of it running in deep ditches, part of it standing so as to form marshes." The Spanish word translated as "ditch" was "zanja," which is the same as that used for the sort of channel which was later dug for irrigation purposes, but in this text it was used to indicate natural streams.

On July 31 the men hacked their way through brush and low woods and were able to cover but half the distance of the day before. They crossed another notably difficult and miry stream and camped within sight of a pass that opened between "low hills to the west."

Considering the history of these erratic streams we can only surmise that one across which the "puente," or bridge, was thrown may have been the San Gabriel, perhaps near Bassett where there was a ford in historic times, or perhaps farther downstream. The second crossing may have been of the Rio Hondo which was then a tributary of the San Gabriel, draining the swamps below El Monte, a short stream but one which is remembered to have contained deep pools.

To have reached the San Gabriel at all had meant crossing the San José Creek below the Puente Hills, but this may have been one of the lesser hazards of the way. Lexington Wash, which has been mentioned as that which was bridged, was probably not a major water course at that time. The pass to the west, "between low hills," could have been the one now threaded by Valley Boulevard, or perhaps another parallel to it, through which traffic now streams between Los Angeles and the San Gabriel Valley suburbs.

After a day of rest, during which mass was said in honor of Our Lady, the Queen of the Angels of Porciuncula, whose feast day falls on August 1st, the men pressed on until they came to a "delightful place" under trees by the banks of a river which they named the Porciuncula. The scouts or explorers, who ranged widely while the rest of the party and the pack train usually traveled on a more direct route, discovered the mouth of a tributary stream a little way to the north. This was the one now called the Arroyo Seco. It was dry, the normal condition for midsummer, but the Porciuncula, the present Los Angeles River, was flowing steadily, probably only to lose itself in the vast marshes which lay between that point and the sea.

The diarists wrote glowing accounts of the plain on either side of the river, of the black, fertile soil and the masses of wild grapes and blooming roses. Father Crespi felt it to be the best site so far discovered for the establishment of a Mission, and saw it as capable of supporting a large settlement. This qualifies him as a prophet, but one who might be considerably surprised could he return to see this no longer exactly delightful spot by the river. The ford by which the Spaniards crossed the river may have been the one at old Downey Street, near the present North Broadway bridge, which spans a concourse of railway tracks and from which can be seen the silhouette of the public buildings in the Civic Center of Los Angeles.

The records of the expedition mention two Indian rancherias, one in the lovely spot where camp was made on the night of August 2nd, another which was reached the next day after traveling "half a league" from crossing the river. This second village was undoubtedly *Yangna*, familiar to every third-grade child in the Los Angeles schools as the predecessor of his home city, although in fact the widespread boundaries of the present metropolis contain the sites of many another similar to it.

Measuring with a radius of half a league from the probable crossing, one can draw an arc extending from the base of Fort Moore hill, now greatly cut back from its original girth, to the Union Station. There are those who place *Yangna* at the intersection of Aliso or Commercial and Alameda Streets but the rancheria there was merely a segregated district, a sad remnant of the original settlement. Where, on this arc, was the prehistoric village?

No doubt there was a time when it would have been possible to pick up well-shaped mortars and arrowpoints from the surface, but now we should have to dig up the Civic Center and surrounding buildings, which seems hardly feasible. In actuality some characteristic items were unearthed during the building of the Union Station in 1939, and considerably more, enough to interest the local newspapermen in 1870, when the historic Bella Union Hotel was rebuilt. This site, between Main and Los Angeles Streets north of Commercial, was cleared for a parking lot in 1940. It is on higher ground and appears to be more typical of the place in which a Gabrielino would have chosen to live.

Reviewing the habits of these people, Arthur Woodward calls attention to the fact that these villages were not built for defense. Moreover, a habitation in which the problem of accumulating refuse defeated all the natural scavengers could be burned or otherwise destroyed, and the owner left free to build another wherever his fancy pointed. With these facts in mind one can agree with Woodward that in all probability *Yangna* lay scattered in a fairly wide zone along the whole arc, and its bailiwick included as well seed-gathering grounds and oak groves where seasonal camps were set up. Reid's estimate of 500 to 1500 huts in such a village seems based on too rosy memories, as Father Crespi described as "large" any village of 200 souls.

The name *Yangna* presents difficulties. Alexander Taylor placed it, with this spelling, on his map of the "tribes." Kroeber's sources gave variants of it as *Iya* and *Weno*, and Swanton places *Wenot* at Los Angeles. The word *wenot* meant river in the Gabrielino tongue. For the variant listed by Kroeber, *Iyakha*, the meaning was given as "poison oak." However, J. P. Harrington's informants gave the native word for poison oak as *oár*, and the meaning of *Jana* (transcribed with the Spanish "*j*" and the nasal "*n*") as "Place of the Salty Earth."

The salty earth, Harrington surmised, could have been a description of alkali, which was sometimes deposited in the lowlands along the river and as often covered over by silt when another winter storm overflowed the land. There is, indeed, a tinge of similarity between *Yangna* and *Engner*, the root name for that other "Place of the Salt," *Engnovangna*, by the salt pools of Redondo.

Harrington's informants placed *Jangna* on the site of the plaza in the Pueblo of Los Angeles. A native of that place, they said, would have been known as an *Javit;* plural, *Javitam*. Incidentally, it might be well to remember to accord to the "*a*" in these titles the dignity of the Spanish broad "*a*" since otherwise the *Yabit*, which is the way a resident of *Yangna* was registered at San Gabriel, loses its true identity.

Victoria Reid, who was the Mission-trained Gabrielino wife of her people's chronicler, the naturalized Scotch-Mexican, Don Perfecto Hugo Reid, is said to have been the daughter of a line of chiefs and was named on the Baptismal Register as a *Comicrabit*. The village, the name of which in its locative form must have been *Comicrangna*, was described as having been "adjacent to the Pueblo." The site of this neighbor of *Yangna's* is unknown. Victoria's first husband, the father of her four children, was Pablo Maria, a *Yutucubit*. A similarity exists between this name and *Hutukngna* on the Santa Ana River, which was listed as "*Jutucunga*" on the register.

Two other names have been handed down for places in the *Yangna* region. *Apachia*, a root-name listed by Kroeber and described by Swanton as having been "east of Los Angeles," sounds curiously similar to *Apatsijan*, the name which Harrington's informants gave to a natural pool which lay near the San Gabriel Mission. *Maungna*, which Reid placed on the "Rancho de los Feliz," can be precisely located. Harrington's informants recalled that it had stood where the first Jewish cemetery was established in Los Angeles. The research of Marco Hellman puts this in Elysian Park, on Chavez Road, in the pleasant glade where the Los Angeles police force now has its pistol range. The meaning of the root, *Mau*, was given as "slow."

No traditional names are recalled for the Hollywood area but archeological surveys discovered sites of villages at the mouth of Fern Dell Canyon on Los Feliz Boulevard and northwest of the intersection on Franklin and Sycamore Streets. No doubt fairly large settlements existed at these points and at others which received water from canyons leading from the Hollywood Hills.

Portolá and his men did not linger in *Yangna* but continued across high ground on a course described as south of west. They made camp that night near a large alder tree and a flowing spring in a marshy place. Costansó mentioned that a deep "ditch" ran southwest from this point, a fact which would seem to confirm Bolton's placing of this camp on La Ballona

Creek, west of the "cienega." This was a region of good springs, and La Ballona in the summer would have met this description.

The "explorers" that day probably had taken a well-marked trail leading directly west to the Brea Pits, a trail better known to us as Wilshire Boulevard. They came into camp that evening with tall tales of having seen "large marshes of a certain substance like pitch." This boiled and bubbled, coming up mixed with water, the water running "to one side and the pitch to the other." The tar was so abundant that the men judged it enough to "serve to caulk many ships."

Earthquakes had continued throughout this crossing of Gabrielino territory. The Spaniards looked toward the Beverly Hills and surmised that the unsteady land and the springs of boiling pitch might be explained by the existence of volcanos in those heights. They did not dream of the skeletons of prehistoric beasts which would be lifted from the tar in generations to come, nor could they have imagined the emotional fires to be portrayed on film by the cinema stars who would one day build their homes in those peaceful uplands.

The total population of a large rancheria was out gathering the harvest of seeds as the expedition passed and on August 4th the newcomers proceeded across other grassy plains, perhaps skirting the highlands which have recently been dubbed the Cheviot Hills. The camp that night was "in a hollow entirely surrounded by hills," where "a good village of friendly and docile Indians" shared the water from two little springs. Costansó recorded that this was "near the seacoast," but as they had traveled not more than six miles this rancheria probably lay near the mouth of one of the canyons which debouch from the Beverly Hills, perhaps one of those which enter the upper reaches of Santa Monica Canyon. Springs in this area are technically seepages at the base of the gravels which form the palisades. In winter small streams would have been running down the canyon.

The scouts continued their exploration to the sea itself and along the beach north of Santa Monica, until steep cliffs cut off further progress. They came back to recommend proceeding by way of a gap in the hills which had been duly noted. This advice was followed and thus white men for the first time crossed these hills into the San Fernando Valley, most probably by the route of the present Sepulveda Boulevard. The Spaniards were captivated by their first view, from the crest of the pass, and enjoyed for two nights a rest by a large pool down in the valley. The large settlement here perhaps marks this spot as having been near the intersection of Balboa and Ventura Boulevards, where an archeological survey located a considerable accumulation of Indian artifacts.

Father Crespi named the San Fernando valley "Santa Catalina de Bononia de los Encinos." There is no record of the name of the populous village by the pool. After the celebration of mass on August 6th the newcomers were entertained by their native hosts, learning from signs and drawings on the ground something of the Channel Islands, of ships that had been sighted off the coast, of bearded Spaniards who had settled in the distant interior. They were given information which filled them with foreboding about some impassable waters which lay to the north, how far ahead they could only conjecture.

On succeeding days the San Fernando Valley was crossed by a route which led a little way to the north of the spot where, 28 years later, the Mission San Fernando Rey was to be founded, the 17th in the order of establishment. Tradition assigns to a village near this site the name *Pasekngna*, and the founding fathers recorded another at the place where they chose to build. *Achois Comihabit* was their version of it, but it has also been transcribed in the locative form, *Achoicomingna*.

Many a modern community in the San Fernando Valley can boast of an Indian predecessor. From Tujunga to Chatsworth archeological sites abound, and a few of them have received systematic excavation. Some were occupied by people of a far more ancient time than those who watched the progress of the Portolá

expedition that summer of 1769. Of the rancherias of
that period we have but a few more traditional names.
There was *Tuhungna* itself, standing along the northern bank of the Big Tujunga Wash, just below Foothill Boulevard, and *Muhungna*, which probably lay in
the verdant lowlands near the mouth of the Little
Tujunga.

The meaning of the root *Tuxu'u* was "old woman,"
possibly an association with some feminine earth figure. On the Baptismal Register of San Fernando the
name appears in the Spanish form, Tujunga, and also
as *Tujubit*. A woman of *Muhungna*, a *Muhuvit*, was
the dubious heroine of the fantasy recorded by Reid,
and reprinted in "The Handbook of the Indians of
California" by Kroeber, as an example of the deliberate
and "artistic incoherence" of this form of literature as
created by the Gabrielinos.

One of J. P. Harrington's informants related a legend of *Muhungna*. He seemed not altogether sure
whether the characters of his story were people, birds
or animals, but with the exception of *Panaxara*, Turtle
Dove, all the inhabitants of this place were treacher-
ously slain. *Panaxara* made her escape only by one
prodigious leap, all the way from San Fernando Valley
to *Pimungna* in the sea, Santa Catalina Island. A comparatively "modern" element in this tale gives the
villains bows and arrows for weapons. After the mas-
sacre one could see, all over the nearby highlands,
"rocks that resemble people, with heads bent as though
fallen where they were shot."

As though to define their exit from Fernandeño
country on August 8th, the Spaniards were forced to
climb and descend the sharpest mountain ridge so far
encountered. The modern motorist, as he sweeps into
Newhall Valley along the wide highway, may recall
the narrow tunnel which once pierced the ridge near
this point. An earlier wagon-wide cut, still visible just
east of the highway, begun by citizens in 1858 and
deepened by E. F. Beale when he was Surveyor-Gen-
eral, reminds the historically-minded traveler of the
struggles of this first cavalcade. Later pioneers used

yokes of oxen and windlasses to bring their wagons over this divide.

Through Newhall Valley and along the Santa Clara River, which the Spaniards reached by way of Castaic, they were in the land of those other Shoshoneans, the Alliklik branch of the Serranos. Here the refreshments offered by the Indians included "a sweet preserve like little raisins, and another resembling honeycomb, very sweet and purging, and made of the dew which sticks to the reed grass." In the Santa Clara Valley the visitors witnessed a native wedding, the bride "the most dressed up among them all in the way she was painted and with her strings of beads."

On the return trip in January, 1770, the San Fernando Valley was crossed from another angle. Coming in from the region of Camarillo on the coast, and being misled by their Indian guide into a maze of canyons in the Santa Monica Mountains, they at last trusted themselves to a second Indian who turned northeast. Just as they were losing their faith in this man they reached a point from which they could see the valley they had first encountered at Encino. This looked like home to the weary men and they spent a night at their old camp by the pool.

The Spaniards had crossed the Gabrielino borderline at a canyon in the Santa Monica Mountains to which they had given the name "El Triunfo del Dulcisimo Nombre de Jesus." This region was to become one of the outlying ranchos of the San Fernando Mission. Searching for a way out of the valley, one more direct and gentle than the Sepulveda Boulevard route, they came upon the pass which was sometimes thereafter marked on maps as "Portezuelo," the "Little Door." This was to become a common name in a region of "little doors" between hills, but at this point it represented an opening better known in our day as Cahuenga Pass.

The various Gabrielino names for the village here have already been discussed, beginning with *Kawengna*, as it appeared on Alexander Taylor's map of the "tribes." A quaint North American rendering of it occurs in Alfred Robinson's "Life in California," the book in which this early pioneer had the intelligence and foresight to include a translation of Father Boscana's *"Chinigchinich."* In these memoirs Robinson told of his jaunt on horseback in 1829 while the "Brookline," on which he had sailed from Boston as supercargo's clerk, was lying in San Diego Harbor. One of the notable places the young man visited was "the glen of Cowwanga."

Portolá tripled his speed on the return journey. The expedition camped to the west of the pass, in Hollywood, where they could look down toward the "cienegas," and continued next day southeast to the river crossing, noting as they passed a view through the gaps in the hills of the great range of snowcapped mountains. One more night in the old camp by the San Gabriel River, then a quick swing through "the mouth of the valley," spurning the climb over the Puente Hills, and they were back at *Hutukngna* on the Santa Ana River, on their way to San Diego and to the beginning of that second expedition which was to establish Spanish control over California.

The Mission Period

When the fourth Franciscan Mission, one to be dedicated to San Gabriel Arcángel, was planned the site chosen for it was *Hutukngna,* on the "Rio de los Temblores." A change of plans brought the founding priests, Fathers Somera and Cambon, over into the San Gabriel Valley instead, yet the memory of the earthquakes of the summer of 1769 persisted and the words "de los Temblores" were never dropped from the title. The Mission cattle brand was designated with a "T" and an "S" entwined.

The founding of the San Gabriel Mission and the celebration of the first mass there took place on September 8, 1771, under a shelter of boughs. A well-kept memorial with a bronze plaque on or very near the exact spot was erected by Walter P. Temple, and a State Historical marker has been placed near it. These can be found, not at the site of the famous Mission church, but at "Mision Vieja," or "Old Mission," the original site chosen by the two pioneer fathers. This was "near the gap of the river" known to us as the Whittier Narrows and the markers may be found about a quarter of a mile northwest of Rosemead Boulevard, at the intersection of Lincoln Avenue and San Gabriel Boulevard. A few years later, probably in early November of 1774 though the date is usually given as 1775, a move was made to the present site where there was a better scope for large-scale agriculture.

"Old Mission" lay in a spot far lovelier than the present scene can suggest. Somewhere nearby, perhaps on the rounded hills where oil wells now pump day and night, lay the Gabrielino village of *Isantcangna*. Men from this settlement helped the soldiers and the muleteers to raise the first rude structures of poles and "tules," and gave their attention to the religious observance.

Probably no buildings of a more permanent character were built at Old Mission, although one old resident believed that the adobe building in which he had been born, and which still stood in 1857, had been used to store ammunition for the guards. Years later a little Mexican village of adobe dwellings grew up nearby and took the name "Old Mission," but this was destroyed in the floods of 1867 and now lies in the rubble behind the new flood-control dam.

The present beautiful church of stone took many years to construct, beginning probably in 1790. It became the crowning feature of a whole community of buildings which served to house the Indian families and the unmarried converts who were called "nuns" and "neophytes," and to shelter the activities that were carried on in the communal life which centered at San Gabriel in the heyday of the Mission period. This later development, however, was a far cry from that day in 1771 when the Indians helped construct the first "ramada," or shelter, of brush and poles. The

Gabrielino baskets of the Mission Period.

chapel and the quarters for the priests, soldiers and muleteers alike were built of materials as flimsy as those from which were formed the huts of neighboring *Isantcangna.*

Around all of the rude structures of "Old Mission" the wondering natives helped to throw up a stockade. So many Indians arrived to view the new establishment that the nervous soldiers of the guard set a limit on the number who could enter at one time, and argued that it would be better to exclude them altogether. This puzzled the Indians and the priests as well, the latter pointing out that though the "heathen" came in multitudes they bore no arms, and that the very reason for the existence of the Mission was to give a welcome to all who would come.

A basis for the uneasiness of the soldiers came to light when the chief of a nearby village came to avenge the honor of his wife, who had been lassoed and raped by soldiers. An unequal battle of arrows against shot ended with the chief's head adorning a pole on the stockade as a warning to all who would resist the conquerors. When the priests learned the truth of the matter the head was restored to the grieving relatives, but the damage had been done. It took some time to induce the natives to return to the chapel, and continuing offenses of the same order tended to dull the notion that there existed anything of value in the new regime.

Long before, in 1602, Father Ascension had been of the opinion that no women should accompany the soldiers who were to occupy California, lest there be "offenses to God." The offenses which actually occurred he had not foreseen. Another of his suggestions, that authority should rest in the hands of the religious, was not followed and throughout the history of the Missions, from the founding of the first in 1769 to the secularization act which dissolved them in 1834, a sort of ideological and economic war was waged between the padres and many of the military and secular officials.

It is difficult to obtain an unbiased view of the Mission period in California. Histories have been written which are founded on well authenticated facts, but with interpretations and stresses so opposed that it is difficult to believe that they describe the same people and the same events. An effort to achieve objectivity in regard to these events can begin by attempting to place them in a context of the centuries in which they took place, rather than to judge them by present standards. Another aid is to be found in the studies made directly from the Mission records, of which those of S. F. Cook are invaluable.

Both the religious and the secular leaders of 18th Century Spain envisioned twin goals. Cross and Crown, Christian mission and military conquest, formed a unity with so little sense of opposing values that the charge of hypocrisy, sometimes made, is largely beside the mark. A solicitude for the welfare of the human soul in the life to come, still quite mediaeval in concept, left little room for consideration of the individual or his bodily comfort during his stay on this temporal earth.

In the organization of a Mission, formed for the twin purposes of saving pagan souls and training good subjects for the Crown, it was felt necessary to raise the primitive technological level of the inmates by substituting the tools and skills of contemporary Spain.

Thus there was destroyed a balanced and integrated scheme of living, but no white man of the time, and few of any other era, would have considered this as worthy of a moment's regret.

That to produce trained specialists, herders and vaqueros, weavers, millers, tanners, cooks, spinners, plowmen, orchardists, stone-masons and brick-makers, *et cetera, et cetera*, meant 'round-the-clock regimentation and complete obedience, voluntary if possible but by coercion if necessary, did not seem unreasonable to the Spaniards. Children must be disciplined, and they looked upon the Indians as children. Discipline of the inmates of an institution, however, must not be confused with methods of conversion.

Cook writes, "At the outset it must be stated unequivocally that neither the plans of the Franciscan

Stone water spout carved by Indians for Mission use.

hierarchy nor those of the political government of New Spain contemplated conversion of the heathen on any other than a voluntary basis. Hence it is not at all surprising that the theory endorsed by Serra, Palóu, Lasuen, and the other early missionaries and the routine actually practiced by them employed no other means of conversion. Any pressure was restricted to legitimate m o r a l suasion. Spiritual arguments, and social or economic inducements extended without recourse to threats or physical compulsion." This should be kept in mind, as sensational episodes of an opposite character, reported in later years, are often thought to represent the spirit of the whole era.

Father Palóu, friend and biographer of Father Junipero Serra, President of the Missions, recounted an

episode which took place on the Santa Ana River just
before the founding of the Mission at San Gabriel. As
the priests approached the Indians showed a truculent
attitude; but they were won over, dropping their
weapons and showing evidence of the most tender concern, when they were shown a painting of the Virgin.
This typifies a way, well understood by many of the
Franciscans and sympathetic to their own Latin tem-
peraments, into the hearts of a people with a strong, if
undeveloped, aesthetic sense. Music, color, ritual afforded the Gabrielino converts real pleasure and opened a new path to religious feeling, already present in
their natures. Those who point out that, considering
the language barrier alone, there could have been no
early intellectual comprehension of the Catholic faith
seem to be stressing the obvious. A considerable effort
was made by some of the fathers, who anticipated this
criticism, to learn the languages and give formal instruction. The success or failure of this effort is difficult to evaluate.

In 1812, in answer to the 36 questions of the "Con-
testacion," Fathers Taboada and Zalvidea replied in
regard to Number Ten, on superstitions: "According
to our observations it seems the Indians have some
superstitions or rather vain practices peculiar to recent converts: but little by little we shall succeed in
removing them." This was from San Gabriel. In San
Fernando Fathers Munoz and Nuez enumerated several of the customs of their charges, such as the use of
body paint and of toloache, passing on to the Spanish
government the explanations given by the Indians,
which contained not a hint of the real symbolism or
of the ancient ceremonial usages pertaining to them.
It will be recalled that compiling answers for the questionnaire may have influenced Father Boscana at San
Juan Capistrano to continue the research which led to
the writing of his invaluable work, *"Chinigchinich."*

Cook's definitive work describes the resistances
which the Mission Indians developed toward the regime which the conquerors imposed upon them, the
physical and psychological backgrounds of those resis-

tances, the means which were used by the religious and
military authorities to soften or to uproot them, and
the relative success of the newcomers in the various
aspects in which their culture conflicted seriously with
that of the natives. Oddly enough one facet, that of religion, which has borne criticism from many commentators, is shown by Cook to represent a successful
assimilation — though perhaps not in the way the
Franciscans had anticipated.

Hugo Reid wrote, in 1852, "They have at present
two religions,—one of custom and one of faith." Cook
does not believe it is possible psychologically to hold
two separate sets of beliefs simultaneously and count-
ers this idea, which he calls the "checkerboard" theory,
with one of fusion of the two religions. He quotes Hugo
Reid and Father Boscana to show instances in which
the Indians modified certain of the teachings of the
Christian religion to fit their own basic patterns of life,
such as finding in the story of Christ a parallel to their
own sufferings. Cook comments "This whole sublima-
tion, even though not consciously formulated, is indica-
tive of a really profound insight on the part of those
often described as little above the level of beasts."

Paralleling the religious instruction and the none too
effective medical work of the priests there existed an
underground, after-dark reliance on the suppressed
native leaders, the old chiefs, *pahas* and shamans. The
medicine man's power over the imagination of the
people dimmed or brightened, not through the steady
pressure applied in order to diminish his authority,
but as he failed to cure the new diseases, or in turn
surpassed the medicines of the priest with his own
knowledge of the ancient lore in regard to common ills.
J. P. Harrington recorded, early in our own century,
the name of a Shoshonean, a Serrano, or perhaps a
Cahuilla, who traveled continuously throughout Southern California curing sick people for 10 and 20 dollars
apiece. He had a large following, possibly not entirely
limited to Indians.

Cook points out that "in the mass the Indians never
assimilated the full significance of Christian ethics in

so far as they apply to social conduct." Their own regulatory precepts had concerned simple amenities which were hardly parallels of Christian concepts of morality. One cannot say, however, that Christian societies have often afforded good examples of these concepts, so earnestly taught by missionaries, and this seems to have been the case in Gabrielino territory.

"In the field of personal relationships, laws, and codes of behaviour, the two systems were mutually exclusive and irreconcilable," Cook continues. "For purely pragmatic reasons, the Indians were forced to make a rapid and very difficult adaptation which cost them dear in lives and suffering." He cites such factors as "over-aggregation," large numbers of people in a limited area as against the native habit of spreading the population in small groups, restrictions in freedom of action which to an Indian is felt as a keen suffering, corporal punishments given by impersonal authorities not apparently connected with the offense or with the victim of the offense, and continuous, repetitious labor not in harmony with the native rhythm of seasonal or immediately necessary tasks.

These Indians had no infectious diseases before the advent of the Spanish and therefore had built up no immunities. With the coming of settlers from Mexico, the first of them colonists for San Francisco led by Anza, the later groups subsidized pioneers for the two early Pueblos founded by the decree of Governor Felipe de Neve, San Jose in 1777 and Los Angeles in 1781, venereal diseases were added to the various "poxes" which arrived with the vanguard of the conquerors. During the worst of the epidemics the bewildered and unhappy padres set up an altar in the infirmary at San Gabriel to expedite the giving of last rites to one after another of these once sturdy people who now slipped into eternity with such quiet ease. Fruit trees were sometimes planted between the rows of graves, and the vineyard long in existence at San Fernando marked such a forgotten cemetery.

Gradually, during the last years of the Mission period, the death rate began to drop. Immunities were

being set up, although the introduction of any new disease might bring on a disaster wherever it appeared.
Pneumonia and tuberculosis were great enemies, probably more prevalent and lethal because of the poor
resistance of constitutions riddled with syphilis. Nevertheless the statistics show this gradual lowering of the
death rate, although seldom again did a writer describe
the appearance and stamina of a Gabrielino in the
glowing terms used by the diarists of the Cabrillo and
Vizcaino expeditions.

As permanent buildings were erected the Indians
from the villages which lay within a limited radius
of each of the Missions of Gabrielino country were
drawn into the communal life of the institution. One
who remained unconverted, still a "gentile," continued
in his native rancheria. There came a time when the
last of these was crowded out of existence. At first there
was simply a gradual diminution of the food supply.
The roving herds of cattle belonging to the Mission and
the growing number of ranch owners must have com-
peted seriously for the crop of wild seeds, while spreading vineyards and fields in later years reduced the supplies of native food still further. The game animals
receded farther into the mountains. Soon hungry "gentiles" sought occupations as house servants and on the
range. In the early years Indians tilled small fields, giving shares to the men who considered themselves the
owners of the land, although the idea of individual
ownership of land was one quite difficult for the villagers to comprehend.

Once an Indian became a "neophyte," as a male
convert was called, he was under restriction. Every
moment of his time was planned and supervised. Hours
for religious observances, for meals, for waking and
retiring, for labor in orchard, field, mill, shop or on the
range were dictated. For the women there were domestic duties, gardening, spinning and weaving.

At night the married couples retired to small houses,
the single folk to dormitories. Quite little girls were
added to the roster of the unmarried females, called
"nuns," who slept together on long wooden benches in

Indian dwellings at San Gabriel Mission.

one large room, the doors of which were locked and unlocked night and morning by the woman in charge. This was a measure felt to be for their protection, although nothing is more certain than the great contribution made to the soaring death rate by these thick-walled, poorly ventilated communal bedrooms, one for men and boys, one for girls and unmarried women. The crowding together of comparatively large numbers of people in such enclosures, which in many of the Missions were served by open drains, was contrary to the native plan of small aggregations of thatched huts, well dispersed and open at door and smokehole to every cleansing breeze.

Conditions varied widely from Mission to Mission, and from time to time. A great deal depended on the character of the individual priest in charge. Under the direction of one who was ambitious or fanatical, or both, great material expansion might occur and the work be organized with efficiency, but this often seemed to go hand in hand with harsh discipline and an enforced austerity. Under such conditions the deep natural resistance the Indian felt to such a regimented life and to specialized repetitious labor was greatly increased.

In spite of the many deterrents to escape and the severe punishments dealt to any tribesman who aided a fugitive, it has been estimated by Cook that at all times an average of one among every 10 inmates was actively planning an unauthorized exit. At San Gabriel, up to 1817, eight and six-tenths per cent of all converts had run away, but from San Fernando only two per cent. A few "renegades" joined the bands of desert Indians who raided outlying ranchos for beef and swift horses, but most of those who escaped fled first to the home village, or if they feared to do so or found them too reduced to support more inhabitants, "took to the hills." Other fugitives returned to the Mission voluntarily, as did practically all those who were allowed short "vacations" to ease their longing for the old surroundings and the native food, a longing which amounted in some cases to an actual physical homesickness.

With the many deaths and desertions, while at the same time the Missions were expanding, planting vineyards and orchards, building mills and granaries, tilling more acres, tending more cattle and sheep, a greater dependence was placed on the military to recruit new converts. Some instances are recorded which would have horrified the earliest missionaries. The increasing resistance of the free Indians toward entering the restricted life in the Mission establishments came at the time of the greatest need for more laborers.

Hugo Reid wrote flatly that a converted Indian "lost caste" among his people, and he cited two villages, *Pasinongna* on Rancho del Chino and *Toibingna* on Rancho San José, whose inhabitants were brought into the fold at San Gabriel by the use of military force. In 1787 Governor Fages reported that the extreme limit of the radius from which pliable converts could be drawn was under 20 miles, and that beyond this distance "from their native heath they will not be baptized or will not remain long in the mission." It may be that the bad feeling which grew up between the coastal villages and those of the interior was due to an attempt to ward off the extension of Mission influence. One result of it was the cutting off of the supply of dried fish from the Pacific waters, a great loss to the inhabitants of the valleys.

In contrast to a regime under which a great austerity had existed in San Gabriel, Reid described a happier time under a later padre, when the rough serge dresses which had been issued to the married women and the "nuns" were replaced by pretty cottons and bright shawls. In this later era the men might sport hats, and silk sashes over real suits of clothing, although at first all of them had been clothed in mere tunics and breechcloths, perhaps quite enough during a period of transition from their native state.

Yet even under happier conditions desertions continued. The Gabrielinos could never quite stomach the regimented scheme of life which seemed to be necessary to save their souls from a hell in which they could never quite believe. Hugo Reid wrote "Hell, as taught them, has no terrors. It is for whites, not Indians or else their fathers would have known it. The Devil, however, has become a great personage in their sight; he is called *Zizu*, and makes his appearance on all occasions. Nevertheless, he is only a bugbear and connected with the Christian faith; he makes no part of their own. The resurrection they cannot understand, but a future state of spiritual existence is in accordance with their creed."

Sisu, as John Peabody Harrington transcribed the word, was the root-name of a place two miles from Azusa, at "San Antonio." His old informant remembered tales about the devil which illustrate the keen irony with which the Gabrielinos lampooned the white man's regard for this figure. Although it had been the Spanish priests who first brought it to their attention these Indians reserved their most satirical barbs for the later North American settlers, whose general contempt, contrasting as it did with the more paternalistic attitude of the Spaniards and Mexicans, must have been hard to bear.

"Below Temescal, east of the Rancho del Chino, was a place, '*Winavit*,' which was called the 'Ranch of the Devil'," the old Gabrielino said. At Chino, the modern town, stood *Wapijangna*, a name which survived in the local term, Guapa. Also on Rancho del Chino was the village on Reid's list, *Pasinongna*, which was founded on the root, *pasi*, meaning that staple food, the "chia" seed, from a sort of sage still found on these hills, the "Salvia Columbariae." Swanton places the latter village as "south-east of Pomona." All of these small settlements and several others could have existed at good watering places on the broad acres of this grant, with room to spare.

When one came from "Temescal" to Chino, while still on the south side of the Santa Ana River, one reached the place at the point of a mountain which was called *Towis Puki*, "the house of the devil."

"The devil used to come out here at night," the old man said. "The Indians would ask the Americans, 'and did you not see the devil?' The Americans did not believe that any devil was there." . . . "About three or four Americans went up by the devil's house and then the devil came out with keys in his hand and the Americans got scared. They decided to set a trap for the devil and caught him. Not knowing what to do with him they decided to send him to Washington, and not knowing what to do with him in Washington they decided to turn him loose again. The Americans who did not believe in the devil all died. The place is called in Gabrielino *Sisu 'a kin*. It may be only a half a mile from Rancho del Chino."

The word *towis* was Luiseño for "devil," yet, as in many of the cultural items which these Shoshonean groups shared, *towis* seems to have been used by the Gabrielinos as a root for quite a number of place names and may have originated with them, as did the basic religion. *Towis* undoubtedly refers to a concept formed long before these people had become acquainted with the European devil.

This word is found in the Luiseño *Chum towi*, meaning "our spirit," and is cited by Benedict in a discussion of the Luiseño "Songs of Death," which are chanted while they burn the clothes of the persons being mourned. During the burning they chant a recitative describing the cremation of *Wiyot*.

"This recitative tells how thin and sick Ouiot grew," wrote Benedict. "Every song of the *Pikmavul* tells about Ouiot and they change from one to the other.

"Then they march around the fire carrying some of the possessions of the dead person, and burn these things, telling how the First People burned Ouiot. Many dance and a few carry the things. Then they stop and sit down for a while.

"They now make an invocation to the sky three times, breathing, groaning indescribable sounds, and put the things on the fire. They sing: 'No towi, no towi, my spirit, my spirit.' These are the songs of Chum towi, our spirit."

Although a late Gabrielino might translate *towis* and *sisu* as "devil" it is probable that he did so either through ignorance of the ancient concepts, or as a part of his general refusal to expose these to possible ridicule. In the ancient religion the "breath," or ghost, was something quite different from *nisun*, the "heart," or soul. The latter never lingered on earth but ascended to the sky to become a planet.

On Reid's list was "Toybipet," located on the Rancho San José, a domain which includes the modern cities of Pomona, La Verne and part of Claremont. The root of this, *tojts*, refers to the "devil woman who was there," living nearby, a *Sisuvit* of the village at "San Antonio." This woman had a child who was not her own. Gopher told the child to run away, and although the woman tried hard to recapture him, he made good his escape. She had very long fingernails and toenails. This woman also was trapped by the white men, but freed by an American government which did not know what to do with her. All this happened "a long time ago."

Another of these names which might have referred to the spirit concept was *Toviscangna*, which shares with *Sibangna*, sometimes recorded on the baptismal records as *Sibapet*, the distinction of having been the settlements closest to the land to which the San Gabriel Mission was moved in 1774, and where the church still stands. *Tuvusak*, a variant of the name *Sibangna*, is listed in Kroeber's "Handbook of the Indians of California."

Father Serra himself penned the title page for the Book of Confirmations, as follows:

Este Mision del Santo Principe
el Arcángel San Gabriel
de los Temblores
alias Toviscanga,
El Cuatro de Noviembre, 1778.

Thomas Workman Temple II has seen in the "Book of Deaths" the name of one Marcos José de Toviscanga, who died on May 7, 1783. This name appears also on the Baptismal Register, entry number 803, dated April 25, 1782.

Temple also found a reference concerning the first child to be baptized at "Old Mission." He was the off-spring of "El Interprete," a man who was the "first to show a few syllables in his native tongue." The birth-place of father and little son was a "rancheria to the east of the mission on a plain entirely surrounded by water on all sides." The chronicler gave the name of this village as *Ouiichi*. On old topographical maps one can make out what might have been such an "island" between what were the swamps below El Monte and the Old San Gabriel River. Here was formed the Mission's Rancho Potrero Chico, a diamond-shaped tract of a little more than 83 acres. Thousands of motorists cross this old site daily on Rosemead Boulevard somewhat north of its intersection with San Gabriel Boulevard.

A settlement which retained its identity into historic times was the one listed by Reid as standing on Rancho La Puente. His spelling of it is *Awig-na*, but it is listed by others as *Ahujvit*, *Ahuingna*, *Ajuinga* and *Ajuivit*.

It is mentioned in the diary of a journey of inspection made by Father Sanchez in 1821. Traveling from *"Guachinga,"* on the Mission Rancho San Bernardino, to San Gabriel, he passed through "Guapia" on Rancho del Chino and the village of "Ajuenga." One early record places *Aguibit* as "right next to Old Mission."

This rancheria, which can perhaps best be transcribed as *Awingna,* existed even after Rancho La Puente passed from Mission ownership to that of John Rowland and William Workman. It lay on the banks of San José Creek, just east of the family cemetery which was established by these men. In this cemetery, still maintained by the present owners, Governor Pio Pico's body was given interment.

A hint that *Awingna* had more than ordinary importance lies in an early record translated by Thomas Workman Temple II. The old text ran, "Matheo, Capitan de la Rancheria Ajuibit, whom the other rancherias regard as their chief, was baptized June 6, 1774, at the age of thirty-five or six." Here was one more of the rare instances in which one man ruled several villages. Being a chief, Matheo was faced with a dilemma which did not trouble lesser men: namely, to make a decision as to which of his wives to retain as his bride in the Christian ceremony which was to follow his baptism. The record gives the name of his choice as Francesca.

Reid's "Toybipet," also recorded as *Toibina* and *Tojvingna,* could have been any one of the several rancherias which existed on the vast Rancho San José. These seem to have been occupied to a much later date than is usual. A survey map of 1874 shows one at the intersection of Towne and San Bernardino Avenues in Pomona. Ganesha Park, south of the Los Angeles County Fair Grounds, was also the site of a flourishing settlement. Another candidate for this traditional name seems to be the village at Mud Springs, near the intersection of Cienega Avenue and San Dimas Canyon Road near La Verne, where a marker commemorates one of the camps of the Anza party of 1774. Another possible contender for this particular title is Indian Hill, north of Foothill Boulevard in Claremont. Two hundred Indians lived there in 1870 and the last to cling to the spot left in 1883.

On a knoll north of the present city of Azusa lay *Asuksangna*. The root of this name was *asuk*, "his grandmother." J. P. Harrington's informant thought the grandmother must have turned to stone, as "there were people everywhere that turned to stone." He added that the phrase "I am an Azusa Indian" would be spoken in Gabrielino, "Non im Asuksavit." This form of the word appears in the Baptismal Register as "Asuesabit."

Winingna was a rancheria which occupied the spot where the city of Covina had its beginnings. The name seems to correlate with the *Guinibit* of the Baptismal Register. All that the old Gabrielino associated with it was the phrase "where there were metates lying about, as in an Indian camp."

One of the traveled roads from the Mission to the Pueblo circled somewhere to the south, keeping to high ground over the present Monterey Pass, often called Coyote Pass. The horsemen from ranchos to the east, such as that of Juan Matias Sanchez of Rancho Potrero Grande, preferred this route. Old residents recalled that carriages traveling to the Mission stopped at "Halfway House" in the pass to rest the horses and give refreshment to the travelers. A profusion of blooms gave this place, and the ranch of 5,000 acres which was formed here by purchase after the Civil War, the name "Rosa de Castilla." The Indians had led in the use of this descriptive title, as the Gabrielino village in this region also had been a "Place of the Roses," based on their word for rose, *otsur*.

The 25 names on Reid's list which refer to mainland "lodges" do not suffice to cover a small proportion of the locations which archeology indicates as having been occupied by Gabrielinos, and it is now impossible to place more than a small percentage of the several hundred rancherias listed in the records of the two Missions. Sometimes a traditional name has been assigned to a given spot, only to find that information acquired at a later time may cast a doubt on its validity.

Indian-made wheelbarrow used at San Gabriel Mission. (From "Index of American Design").

Hugo Reid placed his *"Hahamog-na"* on the "Rancho de los Verdugos." For some years this name has been connected with a spot on the east bank of the Arroyo Seco in South Pasadena, where the Garfias Springs still flow. These springs bear the name of an early owner of Rancho San Pasqual, who acquired it some years after it passed from the control of the Mission.

In reviewing the problem of the location of *Hahamongna* one has first to consider the extent of Rancho San Rafael, which the original owner, José Maria Verdugo, preferred to call "La Zanja." This was a vast triangle, with its apex at the joining of the Arroyo Seco and the Los Angeles River and its broad base below the mountains to the north. The eastern flank lay on the Arroyo and a vague western boundary separated it from the range which was to become the property of the San Fernando Mission. Verdugo was corporal in the guard at San Gabriel. He received permission from the governor to use this land in 1784, and retired to enjoy a pastoral life there in 1799.

The requirements exacted of Verdugo included the

placing on the property of a person who would not in-
jure the Indian residents, or be "exposed" to them, the
payment of an annual contribution of "two hundred
fanegas of grain for the good of the community," and
the erection of a stone house. No trace of such a building, which need not have been larger than one small
room, exists, nor does it seem possible to locate the
exact spot on the Los Angeles River from which his
prized irrigation ditch branched.

The "zanja" marked the heart of this great rancho
in its earliest years. Two other tracts, Ranchos Los Feliz
and Providencia, were served by irrigation ditches
drawn from the same area. This lay near the intersection of the present Forest Lawn and Crystal Spring
Drives, north of Griffith Park. Not too far from this
point the river appeared to have its source, since the
accumulated drainage of the vast upper region came
to the surface here where the valley narrowed.

Father Vicente de Santa Maria visited this spot in
1795 when he was assigned to explore the upper valley
to find a likely spot on which to establish the Mission
which was to be named for San Fernando Rey. He saw
no white men during the four hours which his party
spent at the "Parage de la Zanja," but reported the
existence of "a great field of watermelons, sugar melons,
and beans, belonging to an old gentile named Requi
and to other gentiles of the same class, who live con-
tiguous to the ranch of Verdugo."

In his report, Father de Santa Maria wrote "Here we
see nothing but pagans passing, clad in shoes, with som-
breros and blankets, and serving as muleteers to the
settlers and rancheros, so that if it were not for the
gentiles there would be neither pueblo nor rancho; and
if this be not accepted as true, let them bring proof.
Finally these pagan Indians care neither for the Mission nor the missionaries."—"The whole of pagandom,"
he felt, was "fond of the Pueblo of Los Angeles, of the
rancho of Mariano Verdugo, of the Rancho of Reyes.
and of the Zanja." Mariano Verdugo was the brother of
José Maria, who lived on Rancho Cahuenga, while
Reyes was the settler who gave up his disputed claim

to the land which was chosen for the San Fernando Mission.

First contender, then, for the name *Hahamongna* is a village which stood near the intake of "La Zanja" and was the home of Requi and his fellow workers, who may have been tilling these fields on a share arrangement with Verdugo, as this was a practice sometimes followed in those early days of the Spanish occupation. This placing of that traditional name is confirmed by several records. Swanton places *"Hahamo"* north of Los Angeles, and in a recent translation by Thomas Workman Temple II of an old Spanish manuscript in the Bancroft Library a reference was found to an Indian, a native *Jajamovit*, whose home village lay "three leagues" from Mission San Gabriel, an estimated distance which places it far, far beyond the Arroyo Seco.

John Peabody Harrington transcribed the name with the nasal "n" and the letter "x" in place of the Spanish "j," which is used in the Baptismal Register at San Fernando. His informant said the village was near San Fernando, and gave, as an associated phrase, "They seated themselves there," which draws a picture of a place to rest on a long, hot trail.

Archeological surveys have placed a few of what must have been scores of settlements on the broad acres of the old corporal's princely domain, and undoubtedly the adobe homes built by his descendants were placed with an eye to the water sources which had once supported these ancient settlements. Indian material has been found in quantity in oak-shaded Verdugo Canyon and on either side of what are now the grounds of the Glendale Sanitarium, in the lower reaches of Chevy Chase, and along the west bank of the Arroyo Seco.

Authentic references to traditional villages in the Eagle Rock area seem not to exist, although the springs and vegetation of this T-shaped valley must have made it Indian country *par excellence*. To the modern resident, who perceives at a glance the "eagle" on the face of the great outcropping which gives the valley its present name, it seems incredible that the Spanish called it "Piedra Gorda," or "Fat Rock," and that no record seems to remain of any Indian name for the landmark. It is said that a natural dam once held back a lake in the southern branch of the valley. Excavations for building here brought to light the bones of ancient animals, and artesian springs still well up from the ground. Mortars and other artifacts said to have been found at many points in the valley have long been scattered and lost.

Boy Scout Troop No. 40 of the San Rafael district, a section of Pasadena lying west of the Arroyo Seco on Verdugo land, published in 1955 an illustrated guide to their own area which is founded on excellent research. Among the interesting items to be found in this booklet is the fact that numbers of Indian artifacts were found on a hill above the intersection of San Remo Road and San Rafael Avenue. This is no great distance from the charming little valley which still holds a living reminder of the pools of those earlier days. Johnston Lake, as this is called, was named for Alexander Campbell-Johnston, a distinguished Scot who purchased a great tract of land here in 1882.

The Post-Mission Period

The prevailing simplicity and peace of these early pastoral years, enjoyed by such men as Verdugo, were disturbed as currents of revolutionary feeling began to reach California. Mexico was veering toward a severing of its ties to the Spanish Crown. The date of the actual achievement of independence by Mexico is given as 1822, but long before that even the Indians became aware of changes which affected their obscure lives. It is said that when the new flag appeared they welcomed the sacred figure of the eagle in place of the Lion of Spain.

A sign of the coming upheaval in the distant capital was the failure to receive the customary funds for the support of the often forgotten frontier in upper California. The legal rights of the missionaries were ignored; their stipends became somehow frozen in the "Pious Fund" in Mexico City. Even the provincial government officials began to miss supplies and salaries, and Indians who were ordered to work in the presidios received no longer the pittances which had given this labor a faint aspect of equality.

No one thought of asking a soldier to till a field or learn to make a shoe. The Missions were to be observed, ever apparently more prosperous, with their "neophytes" obviously ordained by Providence to work out their salvation in service to the conquering race. What more natural than to ask the Missions and their charges to make up the deficits in the civil and military budgets?

During the years preceding the achievement of independence the "Mission Indians" assumed, quite without their own awareness or consent, the support of the military. Father Ibarra of San Fernando carried on a long and hot correspondence in regard to the plight of his charges with Captain de la Guerra of Santa Barbara. In July of 1821 Father Ibarra wrote that he was not unwilling to contribute to the support of the presidio, but as father and pastor of these "unfortunate orphans" he did not want to pay in the next life for the damage that negligence on his part might cause. He continued, "I see that not by treating these Indians as slaves will it be possible to meet so many expenses."

In 1825 Father Ibarra complained that the presidio considered it a sacred duty of the Mission to give aid, but he considered it equally incumbent on the soldiers to aid the Mission. The help he desired at this time, however, was resumption of the use of troops "to follow runaway Indians and bring them back."

San Fernando and its outlying ranchos had been from the beginning plagued with rodents and pests. Squeezed between grasshoppers and human parasites the Fernandeños took the short end. Of 100 "fanegas" of beans which matured, roughly 160 bushels, Father Ibarra estimated that 25 to 30 went to the guards, 16 to the presidio, 10 to the civil government; leaving 44 to 49 for all the "Indian creditors, the real owners, those who picked them after they cost them dearly, first on

These longhaired Indians in white man's garb are seen making adobes at a Southern California Mission. (Arthur Barr photo).

account of the labor and care, and then on account of the punishments subjected to."

Soldiers were not supposed to visit the Indian rancherias or to give direct orders to "neophytes" at the Missions. Only certain men, directly detailed to work on the ranges, were allowed horses. The natives walked. Father Ibarra found all of these provisions flouted by the guards and soldiers. In 1821 he wrote of these infringements and their results: "Many of the Indians wear fineries, and they are given to drink. I refrain from saying anything more, for it ought to be communicated face to face. They (the soldiers) also give horses to the Indians; in fact they do just as they please."

At San Gabriel, "Queen of the Missions," nature was cooperative. Although San Luis Rey held the record for the highest average annual yield, the greatest single harvest was brought in at San Gabriel in 1821. Yet, in spite of this apparent prosperity, Cook estimated from a careful study of the Mission records that on the average an Indian living in one of the Missions received an allowance of food somewhat below the caloric value necessary to maintain his working day and good health. This was true even though the labor required was not often what we would class as heavy, and under ordinary circumstances did not exceed a 40-hour week. Nevertheless hunger, mostly of the kind we call "hidden," but in some instances all too apparent, may have contributed to their weakness in combating the imported infectious diseases and to the "laziness" which was charged against them by those who wanted a maximum of service from the aborigines.

This condition perhaps augmented the longing for the native foods of the "good old days." In 1826 Father Zalvidea wrote of insufficient fat, beans and corn for his charges at San Juan Capistrano. On one occasion, 30 years earlier, it had been necessary to send half of the inmates of the San Gabriel Mission "for some months into the mountains to search for food after the manner of the savages." Those remaining went on half rations and a little milk, with meat on certain days, a situation which continued until the wheat was harvested.

In the decade following the gaining of independence by Mexico the pressure against the Missions intensified. Many of the Spanish-born priests refused to sign oaths of allegiance which would have severed their ties with the old country. In 1827 a law was passed to expel all persons of Spanish birth; but few of the old padres were disturbed. They were needed to "control" the Indians. Replacements, however, were appointed from the Mexican priesthood, trained at Zacatecas.

Critics of the Mission system could point to a decree which had been issued in Spain in 1813. Although this had never been enforced, as it had taken some eight years for news of its passage to reach California, it contained provisions that were continued to be urged by the leaders in the movement to secularize the Missions. It provided that all Missions in the Americas, when they had been in existence for 10 years, were to receive the status of parish churches under local bishops. The friars would then be appointed as temporary curates or be moved to the new frontier to set up new Missions. The land was then to be distributed to private ownership and the Indians, presumably to be numbered among the landowners, were to be governed by civil authorities.

A plan envisioning the formation of pueblos to be inhabited by Indians living near each of the Missions went into effect at three of them in 1833. One of these was set up at San Juan Capistrano, but the pueblo is said to have been a failure due to the "apathy, indolence, and incompetence" of the Indians who comprised its citizenry. To judge by surviving Juaneños, who are healthy, kindly and quick-witted people, there must have been considerable eagerness to take every advantage of lack of preparation, experience and guidance during the short-lived experiment. At any rate, the titles to the lands soon found their way into the strongboxes of white men. For many years the Juaneños clung to their "jacales" along the hillcrests above the Mission, then most of them scattered out to find employment.

A distinguished Englishman who visited California in 1831, Dr. Thomas Coulter, returned to London to write and lecture on what he had seen. This astute observer wrote, after speaking of the prolific livestock to be seen on the range, "The number of white inhabitants has also increased very rapidly, and I believe is now not under six thousand, though I cannot state their numbers very exactly until I shall have examined the statistical material which I have collected.

"The reverse, however, is the case with the original inhabitants. They have diminished considerably in number, though in this case, one would suppose they ought at least not to have lost ground, not having been driven from their homes as in the United States, nor having had ardent spirits at all within their reach until lately. But they have been compelled to live under a restraint they could not bear, and to labour a little— neither of which they would submit to if they could possibly avoid it. Though the fact is as far as possible dissembled, I believe a great deal of both force and fraud were used in congregating them together in the missions; and the moment that force shall be altogether withdrawn, I have no doubt that the majority of them will return to the woods. Now that the seaboard is pretty much occupied by whites, the Indians will probably retire to their relations still living free in the interior.

"It is a very extraordinary fact that their decrease is greatly hastened by the failure of the female offspring —or the much greater number of deaths amongst the females in early youth than among the males—I have not been able clearly to determine which, although the latter appears more probable; the fact, however, of there being a much smaller number of women living than men is certain. Infanticide, properly so-called, is not common, though very frequent recourse is had to the means of producing abortion, chiefly mechanically, but this will not account for the state of things described as males and females must be supposed in this way to suffer equally . . ."

Coulter went on to say that the spirit of the Spanish laws was to afford the Indians protection, so that for a while they might keep their ancient possessions, but that they would in the end lose, due to a combination of their own vices "to which they cling, and to those of their neighbors which they easily acquire." He expected annihilation of the entire aboriginal population because he found few traces of "moral energy" among them.

Coulter was a keen observer, but his comments show the typical blindness of the white man toward Indians. A little use of his imagination would have told him that no tribe of lazy men and women could have survived in this area, as the self-directed Gabrielinos had done with singular success. He did not see that long years of regimented life had systematically rooted out the Indian's own variety of initiative and enterprise, which had made a balanced use of the land without depleting or destroying its resources.

The Englishman made a distinction, far too delicate, between being driven from one's land and having it taken from beneath one's feet. There had been a time when no Gabrielino was under the necessity of "retir-

ing" to non-existent relatives "in the interior." It must
be admitted, that those seen by Coulter were people
much weakened by the diseases of their conquerors.
Many were mixed bloods, although until punishment
ended the practice resistance to this form of encroach-
ment had taken the form of abortion.

As to the lack of "moral energy," it must be remembered that everything which had held these people in
the matrix of an effective tribal organization had been
taken from them. Language, oral literature, song, ritual,
native leaders, all had been suppressed or eradicated.
The incentives to work, which in their native state had
been induced by their leaders through seasonal, ritual-
istic and collective drives, or lay in such a goal as a
single piece of handicraft well-wrought, could not be
recaptured in tasks imposed by the conquerors. Indeed,
the society of the time, that of the "gente de razon,"
was not based on specialized industry of the sort organized by the padres, that repetitious labor to which
the Indian, who had lived close to his earth and who
possessed an artistic feeling for the materials of the
earth, opposed the weight of his passive and largely
unconscious resistance.

Father Duran wrote in 1831, "It would be better with
less bluster about the Indians to begin with the *gente de
razon*. Let the latter begin to work, to found establishments and schools, and to practice arts and industries:
then will be time to lead the Indians to follow the
good example."

Father Duran also faithfully adhered to the thesis
that the Indians, though still "children" and in need of
the fatherly control of the priests, were the absolute
owners of all Mission property. Father Zalvidea had
carried their title back to the time when, as he thought,
the Jews had wandered across the Bering Strait to become the ancestors of the American Indians. He based
his naive ethnological viewpoint on his own interpreta-
tion of the writings of the prophet Ezra.

It may be possible that Father Zalvidea was somewhat of a prophet himself, trying in a few years to
bridge the cultural gap between his charges and the

masses of immigrants which the turn of history was bringing into their lands. This might explain, at least in part, the severity with which, during his regime at San Gabriel from 1806 to 1827, he drove the Indians and himself in the building of the physical development of that Mission. This great zealot desired "to be relieved of the temporal government of the Indians," and felt that the decree of the Court of Spain of 1813 should have been enforced.

The "gentile" Indians had their own difficulties. Work on the ranchos also took the form of repetitious drudgery. Payment was seldom thought necessary. Food, cast-off clothing and a spot to build a shanty seemed enough in a land where the rancheros themselves saw little cash, their only marketable products being hides and tallow. Later, as the demand grew for the potent grape brandy, the workers in the vineyards sometimes received small sums. It became more convenient, however, to give wages in liquid form, simple barter of a week-end of forgetfulness of pain and frustration for six days of labor. Sometimes for a favor, or for a trifling sum, an Indian found himself bound to give an entire year of service.

In the Pueblo the most menial work fell to the lot of the Indians. They lived in squalor in a segregated district and for a minor offense, one quite ignored when committed by one of the *"gente de razon,"* a man could be bound over a cannon and given a hundred lashes. This was at a time when officials were expressing great concern over the severity of the punishments in the Missions which, theoretically at least, were limited to 25 lashes for a major crime. Some rather cynical evasions of this ruling did occur, yet the loudest critics of the Missions in this regard were prone to overlook the common practices of the civil authorities.

When secularization actually went into effect in 1834 the legal background of the decree which brought it about was involved and obscure. The action of the California legislature was repudiated in Mexico in 1835, but by that time the Missions were well on their way toward dissolution and this movement merely gained momentum after secular commissioners took over the control. Theoretically the Mission lands and property belonged to the Indians, but, as usual, no one consulted with them as to their disposal. The incredible fact seems to be that the liquidation of the assets of these institutions began even before the authority of the priests was superseded by that of secular commissioners.

The extensive slaughter of the Mission herds was supposed to have been done on shares, with the Indians receiving a portion of the profits, but the contractors appear to have hoodwinked the priests and to have retained the lion's share. Utensils, tools and other goods were distributed and even the roofs of the Mission buildings were torn off to be used as firewood. Irrigation ditches were left to deteriorate.

Hugo Reid wrote of this phase, "It did not require long to destroy what years took to establish. Destruction came as a thief in the night. The whites rejoiced at it. They required no encouragement and seemed to think it would last forever. Even the mere spectators were gladdened at the sight, and many helped themselves to a sufficiency of calves to stock farms."—"Administrator followed administrator," Reid continued, "until the Mission could support no more, when the Mission system was broken up."

In 1843 certain of the Missions, including those of San Fernando and San Gabriel, were restored to the control of the priests, but the property by that time included only the church buildings and the surrounding orchards. The remaining "neophytes" and the padres were expected to eke out a precarious income of which one-eighth was to be paid into the public treasury.

During the 1840s the fertile Mission ranchos were parceled out to individual ownership. Few were the acres which fell into the hands of Indians. The phrase which justified this distribution, "lands not required by the neophytes," was based on a cynical brand of realism, for with the despoiling of the Mission properties great numbers of the inmates had scattered, not waiting to ask for land, not knowing of their right to it, and unable to have used it to advantage.

Of the ranchos which actually were ceded to natives the larger tracts seem to have been in the San Fernando Valley. El Encino was given to three, formerly neophytes of the Mission, but was sold by them within a few years. Of another trio, who acquired Rancho El Escorpion, one bought out the interest of his partners and then disposed of the property to relatives. Samuel, a Fernandeño who was allowed the use of a substantial acreage, sold his interest in the early 1860s. José Miguel Triunfo traded his grant of the nearly 400 acres of Rancho Cahuenga for the more than 4,000 which comprised Rancho Tuhunga, and then sold the latter in 1850.

The few Indian grantees of San Gabriel disposed of their comparatively minute holdings as promptly as did their brethren of San Fernando. The slightly more than 23 acres known as the Prospero Tract are now included in the grounds of the Huntington Library. A patent was issued to the Gabrielino, Simeon, for a little over 30 acres in 1876, and another to one Domingo for his somewhat more than 22 in 1871. These patents were the results of reviews of their titles by the Land Commission of the United States. Yet Domingo's tract had been sold, and resold, before the patent was issued.

Of the other many thousands of acres which had belonged to the San Gabriel Mission only the foregoing, and the 128 of the lovely "Huerta de Cuati," were ceded to the charges of the padres there. This name seems to be a mixture of Spanish and Gabrielino, "*Huerta*" meaning "garden," and "*Cuati*," which may perhaps have been a Spanish rendition of the Indian word, "*quiote*," which meant "*agave*" or century plant. This grant was made to Victoria of *Comicrangna*, the Mission-trained Gabrielino wife of the adventurous Scot, Hugo Reid.

One of the great ranchos, San Pasqual, became for a time the property of Juan Mariné when he was newly married to the elderly widow, Doña Eulalia Perez de Guillen, who had served the Mission long and faithfully as housemother and midwife. The governor's favor in the matter was in the nature of a reward for the

wife's devotion to her task, but when Mariné died she
was left with only a house and a garden in San Gabriel.
The Mariné heirs failed to establish their claim and
Rancho San Pasqual fell to successive owners, until in
1875 a great share of it became the city of Pasadena.

Hugo Reid is said to have met Victoria when she was
living with Doña Eulalia as her protege on Rancho San
Pasqual. No doubt her husband, Pablo Maria, a Yutucubit, lived there also, but some two years later he died
of smallpox. Reid's biographer, Susanna Bryant Dakin,
suggests that Reid's departure from California may
have been motivated by a resistance to his feeling for
the young Indian woman, as he returned soon after she
was widowed and very shortly became a Catholic, a
Mexican citizen, the husband of Victoria and stepfather
for her quartet of Gabrielino children. He applied for
title to the great Rancho Santa Anita and in due time
received papers for provisional and then for outright
ownership.

The furor over this marriage died down as Victoria
proved to be a gracious hostess, presiding with dignity
over well-appointed households. The first of these was
a two-storied adobe residence in San Gabriel, and the
second the adobe on Santa Anita. The latter has been
restored to resemble its appearance in 1839 when Reid
built it. The land on which it stands, a small portion of
the once vast rancho, is now known as the Los Angeles
State and County Arboretum.

Increasing numbers of people are taking the guided
tours of the Arboretum for their botanical and historical interest. The era of one of Reid's successors, Elias J.
Baldwin, the famous "Lucky Baldwin," is illustrated in
the exquisite "Queen Anne Cottage" and the Carriage
House, where Baldwin's fine horses lived in style. Baldwin's additions have been removed from the adobe and
some fairly characteristic Gabrielino wickiups have
been constructed nearby as examples of the architecture
of an earlier day.

"*Aleupkig-na,*" as listed by Reid, is the only one of
the "lodges" on his list which he placed on his own
Rancho Santa Anita, although not a few other Gabriel-

ino settlements existed on 13,000 acres of his original domain. Hugo probably followed the procedure of naming the traditional village nearest the ranch house itself, and no doubt he himself knew where it was, or had been in pre-Mission times. At present, however, the exact location of *Aleupkingna* is just one more archeological puzzle, perhaps to be solved by future excavations on the grounds of the Arboretum, perhaps to remain a mystery.

One of J. P. Harrington's informants pronounced the name *"Ahupkina,"* with the nasal "n," and gave an associated phrase, "where the wind enters to your heart and you inhale wind to cool off." The shade of the great oaks on the knoll to the west of the adobe might well have given rise to such a memory, and Indian material has been found there in sufficient quantity to place that spot in the competition for the traditional name. However, there are other contenders, notably one on the crest on which the greenhouses stand, and another which received a disastrously thorough excavation by means of bulldozers during the construction of the parking lot of Santa Anita Park, the racing establishment which lies to the east of the Arboretum on land that was also only a portion of the great rancho for which it was named.

For the colorful details of the life of Don Perfecto Hugo Reid it is necessary to turn to the work of his biographer, Susanna Bryant Dakin. Her book, "A Scotch Paisano," is based on facts, cleverly and imaginatively filled out to present a rounded story, and it is made the more valuable by the inclusion of that extraordinary source material, the famous "Letters" to the "Los Angeles Star," written in 1852, the last year of Reid's short life.

Reid had been a member of the constitutional convention for the new State of California, and had labored with but small success to insert provisions into the basic law which would protect the rights of the Indians. No doubt, had he lived, he would have continued to use his considerable influence on behalf of his wife's people.

Victoria Reid lived on to 1868 only to die of smallpox, which had taken one after another of her Indian friends and relatives. Hugo had sold Santa Anita in 1846 and she was forced by the straitened circumstances of later years to sell her smaller grant, Huerta de Cuati. Even the house which Reid had built in San Gabriel for his bride was taken from her by the United States Land Commission, due to a shaky title to the land it stood on. The ground itself proved quite as unsteady. Victoria's intense fear of earthquakes, which had prevented her from using the second floor, was vindicated when in 1855 one of the seven giants she believed supported the world stumbled a bit and the entire building collapsed.

Several interesting accounts of life in San Gabriel are to be found in the reminiscences of Laura Evertsen King, written for the Historical Society of Southern California. As a small girl Mrs. King had survived a hazardous crossing of the continent and her acquaintance with Doña Victoria began shortly after the death of the latter's only daughter, the lovely and socially popular Maria Ygnacia. "Lalita" was taken to the heart of the bereaved mother. Her memories spanned the years of the slow decline in the fortunes of the Indian woman, from the years when she dressed in fine silks and wore the jewels Hugo brought her from his travels to a time when, in shabby cotton, she walked with the same dignity and grace that had always made her a striking figure.

The American Period

A major engineering work recently completed in the San Gabriel Valley was the construction of an immense storm drain running down through the Los Angeles State and County Arboretum to join the one already in use under Santa Anita Park. With the covering over, in this fashion, of one more of the natural streams from the mountain canyons it is more than ever difficult to picture this land as ever having been anything but arid. Yet 70 years ago the State Engineer reported four to five hundred acres of wet, marshy land on Rancho Santa Anita and three groups of springs. The parking lot of the famous racetrack quite obscures the original state of that land, although the lake on the grounds of the Arboretum gives proof of the underground waters there.

One of J. P. Harrington's informants told him that there had been no Gabrielino villages in Pasadena; it was all "puro llano," entirely a plain. One might think that the old man's memory was at fault until one considers that the Pasadena of this man's younger days had been that "colony" of North Americans whose homes and orange groves lay well up on the alluvial land which spread in a great fan below the San Gabriel Mountains.

A consideration of the location of Indian sites in this area reveals a garland of habitable spots, lying in a vast curve from Monrovia, around Raymond Hill in Pasadena, and northward along the banks of the Arroyo Seco. The people of these villages undoubtedly used the arid slope above them as an immense wild grain field, going out in season to beat the seeds from the thick native plants into their flat baskets, made for the purpose.

The more one observes the pattern of settlement in this region, which takes in San Marino and Arcadia, the more it becomes apparent that some hidden geological factor entered into its formation. All along this great crescent are found evidences of the breaking of the even slope of the grasslands, such as sharp escarpments cut by glens and canyons, and numerous signs of old streams, pools and marshes.

The North Americans who settled here found that wells sunk below a certain line would be unrewarding, while those above it gushed freely. The first subdivisions and towns were made possible by piping water from the numerous springs along this line or by pushing horizontal tunnels back into the bluffs to tap the waters held in what proved to be an immense bed of gravels, a veritable underground reservoir.

The factor which brings to the surface the waters stored in these gravels is called by the geologists the

"Raymond Dike." Some of the more astute of the settlers of the region kept records of the natures of the
clays which were brought up in drilling wells along
this ancient fault. The Indians had chanced upon the
place as it had been left by nature, lush with pools and
marshes, while the Mission fathers had used water
from the streams which ran down the glens toward San
Gabriel to turn the wheels of the mills which ground
meal or sawed planks for Mission use, and to irrigate
gardens and orchards.

Archeological sites abound along this beneficent, hidden dike, and it is probable that many more existed
than are presently known. The Baptismal Register contains many a name for which no location is known,
and writers, telling of the early days of the city of Pasadena, mention the almost daily gathering of surface
artifacts during the last quarter of the 19th Century.

Most of the Indian material gleaned in this way was
scattered and lost many years ago, and with it went
many an item of information about the life of the
Gabrielinos. However, an unusually large proportion of
the colonizers of Pasadena were professional men, teachers and scientists in various fields, with a bent toward
archeology rather advanced for their time. Some of the
"collections" were not altogether wasted, as in some
cases descriptive lists were compiled which contain valuable information.

Artifacts have been found west of Monrovia near
Foothill Boulevard and on a knoll north of the town,
and others were unearthed during the preparation of
the gardens at the Huntington Library. Tradition places
rancherias above the glen at Oak Knoll, and in other
nearby spots, and beside a brook which once flowed to
the east of Raymond Hill. Thousands of motorists sweep
each day around this hill which rises above the Pasadena Freeway, with a glance perhaps for the apartment
houses at its crest, but without a thought of the famous
hotel which once stood there, and certainly without
knowing anything of the brook and the Indian huts of
still earlier days—a memory quite buried under the
concrete.

From the upper floors of the great hotel the fashionable folks of the '90s could see the ships in the roadstead off San Pedro, and from below the gardens the flow of underground waters is reported to have been audible. This sound probably did not indicate the existence of a mysterious underground river, as was imagined, but the presence of a man-made tunnel bored through the dike to tap the gravels for domestic water.

The dike makes a northward swing along the east bank of the Arroyo Seco, as far as the bluff overlooking the lower end of Brookside Park in Pasadena. This formation and others farther north along the banks of the stream account for the presence of many a spring both above and below the present Devil's Gate dam.

Tradition places a village of Gabrielino Indians at Garfias Springs on Rancho San Pasqual, on the east bank of the Arroyo Seco in Pasadena, and another along the Linda Vista palisades to the west. A concentration of Indian material was found here, south of Lida Street and on the grounds of the grammar school nearby and the whole region was for many years called "Indian Flats."

Another spot which yielded large numbers of items for early collections was on the Gidding's Ranch above Millard Canyon. On the bluffs along the western bank of the Arroyo, above the Rose Bowl, and down in the valley as well, many artifacts were found. As late as 1955 excavation for a home on La Cresta Drive, just off Arroyo Boulevard, brought to light stone objects of Indian origin. This is a region in which such occurrences were common not many years ago.

In 1938 the Southwest Museum conducted a "dig" in this neighborhood at a place which was called the Sheldon Reservoir Site. The material found here proved to belong to a period far earlier than that of the Gabrielino occupation. A report of this excavation appeared in the book "Five Prehistoric Archeological Sites in Los Angeles County, California," by Edwin Francis Walker, published by the Museum in 1951 as Volume VI of the works sponsored by the Frederick Webb Hodge Anniversary Publication Fund.

One of the earliest subdivisions of Pasadena, the "San Gabriel Orange Association," in order to provide water for the homes and groves which were springing up on the grassy slope pumped it from "Sheep Corral Springs" to a reservoir on the high point above the Arroyo Seco, a point which may be roughly described in modern terms as being near the curve of Orange Grove Avenue, somewhat north of Colorado Street. In excavating for the reservoir here Indian material was found at a depth of four feet. A great many of the items discovered were carried away as "curios" or "relics," but enough was retained by the intelligent amateur archeologists among the settlers to give them a comparison with artifacts which were being gleaned almost daily from the surface sites which ringed the uplands of Pasadena.

Hiram A. Reid, M.D., who was not a relative of Hugo Reid, gave a talk on February 27, 1874, before the Pasadena Fortnightly Club in which he described the material found at the Orange Grove Reservoir site as of a very early culture, pre-dating that of the Gabrielino period by an unknown but extended period of time. Some of the items found in the excavation were placed in the Throop Museum, Throop Polytechnic Institute, which later became the California Institute of Technology.

Dr. Reid became the author of a history of Pasadena which contains some excellent source material on the early days of the community and the natural history of the region. He had access to the "Letters" of Hugo Reid and used them in writing of the prehistory of the region. Paradoxically, however, much more knowledge of Gabrielino culture is available today than was the case during the last decades of the 19th Century, when there were surviving Indians who could have been consulted. Writers of that period actually illustrated books on the local natives with pictures of Gabrielinos in Plains Indian war-bonnets, *a la* Sitting Bull.

Dr. Reid placed the Indian village of "Hahamog-na," as transcribed by Hugo, on the San Pasqual side of the Arroyo Seco, whereas the latter gave its location clearly as having been on Verdugo land. He also described the

chief of the Garfias Springs group as having smoked
the peace pipe with Portolá, although the custom was
not true to the Gabrielino culture, and it is improbable
that Portolá saw the Arroyo at this point. The description of Portolá's route, as given by Dr. Reid's history,
fails at several crucial points to coincide with directions
and distances recorded in the diaries of the expeditions.

Of traditional names for many Indian settlements
which followed the Arroyo Seco-Raymond Dike lines
we have but a few. Hugo Reid listed four: *Aleupkingna*
on his own Rancho Santa Anita, *Acurangna* by "La
Presa," *Sisitcanongna* at "Pear Orchard," and *Sonangna*
on "Mr. White's Farm."

Careless research has credited the last of these, *Sonangna*, with a location at Sierra Madre, because a Mr.
Irving White developed a community there. However,
this occurred long after the death of Hugo Reid and
the "Mr. White" of Reid's list was none other than
Michael, that "Miguel Blanco" who had arrived from
England or Ireland in 1829 and who owned for a time
the "Rancho Muscupiabe," named for a Serrano village in the Cajon Pass where the ranch was situated.

Writing of this early pioneer, H. D. Barrows said,
"Mr. White obtained a concession of five hundred varas
square, just north of the mission, which contained inex-
haustible springs of living water." On these 77 acres of
one-time Mission land, which White later sold, he
established a vineyard, an orchard, and an adobe home.
The building still stands at the edge of the athletic
field of San Marino High School and anyone who
goes there can visualize the setting of *Sonangna*, though
it takes a feat of the imagination to erase from the
scene the concrete boulevards, the clipped lawns and
modern buildings, and substitute the natural pools and
cienegas, the native grasses and shrubs, and the great
oak groves which must have supported the *Sonavitam*
in the best Gabrielino style.

One can find the term "La Presa" still in use as the
name of a street which bisects Huntington Drive in a
strip of Los Angeles county land lying between San
Marino and Arcadia. Between this street and San Ga-

briel Boulevard, on the north side of Huntington, there still exists a remnant of the stone dam, or *"presa,"* which was built there in Mission times to impound water to irrigate the fields and vineyards of the region.

No doubt there had been a natural marsh and pool at this place, since this was the neighborhood which supported the village of *Acurangna.* It is known that Indians clung to this old site, or perhaps returned to it after secularization of the Missions, since from a little settlement here came the workers hired by L. J. Rose after he purchased in 1861 the portion of Rancho Santa Anita which became his famous Sunny Slope Ranch. The name of the ancient village had been based on the Gabrielino word *akura,* meaning wood, and it was remembered by an old Indian as a place "where there was plenty of firewood." Mr. Rose himself sold many a cord of it from his vast acreage, yet even in our time one gets an impression of a veritable forest of the great Engelmann oaks, lending to the modern homes beneath their shade a look of unusual charm and permanence.

It has been said that the waters from "La Presa" flowed southwest to turn the wheels of the second of the Mission mills, the one built by Joseph Chapman in 1823. This mill stood a little way to the south of the church building, below the present railway tracks. To divert water to it from "La Presa" would have been quite impossible since a ditch leading in that direction would have had to make a diagonal crossing of the deep channel of the Rubio Wash, which is still to be seen where it crosses Huntington Drive and again where it slashes down through the greens of the present San Gabriel Country Club.

Mr. Dan Mulock, of San Gabriel, whose father bought the Domingo and Salas tracts north of the Mission in 1865, can recall the course of the ditch which actually brought the water to this second mill. It can now be observed by driving southward from the campus of the California Institute of Technology, beginning on Arden Road. The stream which ran here through Wild Grape Canyon was joined by one from San Marino Canyon, now within the grounds of the

San Gabriel Mission from the pond known to the Gabrielino
Indians as Apatsijan. (C. C. Price photo)

Huntington Library. After a wide meander the way
led due south, through the present grammar school
grounds south of Huntington Drive and along a course
parallel to Bridge and Mission Streets in San Gabriel.
After turning the millwheels the stream curved about
below the Mission and filled the hollow to the southeast
of the church, forming a pond seen in old photographs.

Hugo Reid was told that in earlier days, before this
mill was built and the "ditch" leading to it was deepened, the water was free "like everything else to meander where it pleased." It came down to the fertile
hollow nearest the Mission on "the Angeles road,"
through a great oak forest, he wrote, into a massive
thicket "formed of sycamores, cottonwood, larch, ash,
and willows: besides, brambles, nettles, palma christi,
wild roses and wild grapevines lent a hand to make it
impassable, except where footpaths rendered entrance

to its barrows more easy of accomplishment." Reid embellished this description of San Gabriel in the 18th Century with a reminder of the deer that had sported in the neighborhood, and the innumerable bears which had prowled in the thickets. Thus we can visualize the setting of *Sibangna*, which Hugo placed definitely at San Gabriel.

North of the Mission and south of the present Huntington Drive, along this important ditch lay "Pear Orchard," capitalized thus by Hugo Reid. That a large number of Indians once made this their home is proved by the great accumulation of artifacts found on the land which the Mulock and Cooper families purchased here. No name resembling "Sisitcanog-na," the village which Reid assigned to this spot, can be found on the list which Father Sugranes compiled from the Baptismal Register, a fact which makes it necessary to seek for a variant which might have been used in the early days of the Mission.

Being practically on the doorstep of the establishment at San Gabriel, and having a large population, the rancheria which was superseded by the Mission pear orchard was far too important not to be on the record in some form. The probability has to be faced that this was *Toviscangna* itself. This famous name does not appear on Reid's list, but it was used by Father Serra on the title page of the Book of Confirmations. It occurs on the roster of Father Sugranes in Spanish form as *"Tobizcanga."*

The clue which points to this solution is again the interchange between the Gabrielino words *towis* and *sisu*, meaning "spirit" but translated as "devil." The endings *kingna, cangna,* and *canongna* seem to have referred to "houses," probably indicating fairly large settlements. Thus it is possible to translate this name as "Houses where Dwells the Spirit," and at the same time give a possible answer to the puzzle of the location of the two villages given by different authorities as having been situated near the Mission. There still remains the odd similarity between Swanton's *Apachia* and the name of the lake below the Mission. There may have been quite a complex of settlements in that area. It was a rich and well-watered land.

The first of the two mills erected for the use of the Mission, a massive and well-designed building of masonry and adobe brick, still stands on Old Mill Road. This has been for many years a private residence, now almost hidden behind trees and surrounding houses.

Even today a drive from lower Lake Street in Pasadena down Kewen Canyon into the region of Old Mill can somewhat recapture a feeling for the aboriginal beauty of the great crescent above the hidden Raymond Dike. At some points swamps began only a little south of California Street. From the marshes of lower Euclid Avenue a brook flowed to join the stream from Los Robles Canyon. The water for Old Mill came from Mill and Los Robles Canyons through a ditch which led it into the cistern. After flowing through the brick arches of the wheel chambers a concrete channel led it along the face of the escarpment and down into a lake in the valley a little to the southeast.

To those who imagine this to have been an arid land with an undependable water supply it comes as a surprise that many residents of our own day recall this lake, and that some can remember being shown the ruins of the ditches. Many of the springs which the Indians knew still flow. Old Mill was not abandoned because of the fickleness of the water supply but because of the dampening of the ground meal by misdirected sprays. When the beautiful old building was remodeled in the 1920s an active spring beneath the lower floor had to be adequately drained and capped.

The lake also has been drained and one can now enjoy the experience of walking on its old bed along the curving paths of Lacy Park in San Marino. The masses of tules and cattails have been replaced by rose gardens, and the great boulders which the Indians brought here to dam and enlarge the natural pool for Mission uses are no doubt still hidden under the gardens of the surrounding residences. The history of this area is told in outline by the successive names which were given to the lake: Mission Lake, Wilson Lake, Kewen Lake, and now Lacy Park. At least a portion of it passed to the ownership of Benjamin D. Wilson when he purchased from Doña Victoria Reid the Huerta de Cuati. He named his holdings in this neighborhood "Lake Vineyard."

Robert Glass Cleland's small, compact book, "El Molino Viejo," gives the reader a comprehensive view of the first mill and its surroundings, of the life for which it was a center during successive generations, and of the inevitable legendry which has curled its tendrils around the sober facts. Of the period of the 1860s Cleland wrote, "A good many Mission Indians still lived in the vicinity of Old Mill, on sites so rich in Indian relics that a foreman of the Kewen Ranch once filled a four-horse wagon with mortars, pestles, and other artifacts."

Among the many collections of material found along the Raymond Dike and the Arroyo Seco, one of the most notable was made by H. N. Rust, who had brought with him from his home in the East a great number of objects from other Indian cultures. This entire collection was sold to a Chicago buyer and exhibited there during the World's Fair in 1893. It contained fine examples of the now extremely rare Gabrielino basketry.

Charles Frederick Holder, the zoologist and sportsman who wrote such interesting accounts of the Channel Islands, began his comments on the local scene with a book on Pasadena published in 1889. It is notable for its description of the surrounding country, as he explored it before the days of the automobile. He mentions the collection made by Rust and also the fact that there still lived in San Gabriel a fine basketmaker who had learned the art from her grandmother, a famous maker named Laura, who was among those Gabrielinos who survived the epidemics and lived to extreme age, in this case reputed to have been 117 years.

Of Hugo Reid's list of the Gabrielino rancherias we have discussed all but two. Of these *Cucamongna* still retains the Spanish form of its original name. According to archeologists who have observed the area it was probably located east of Red Hill, along the creek in the

A Mission Indian survivor. (From the George Wharton
James collection).

region of the modern town of Cucamonga. A tradition
remains that the meaning of the name was "Sandy
Place." The Indian settlement here was gradually displaced by expanding vineyards.

"*Houtg-na*," as Reid transcribed the name of the village which he placed on the "Ranchito de Lugo," lay

in the vicinity of El Monte. Associated with the name *Hukngna* in the memory of one of J. P. Harrington's informants was a phrase, "in the weeping willow trees." The Gabrielino word for willow is *saxat* and a village in the San Bernardino area, *Saxangna,* was based on that root. Here only the Spanish name El Monte refers to the thickets that bordered the swamps and streams. The old man who recalled this place seemed to be referring to an incident which had occurred in his father's time. "They lashed the Indians much for that," he said, but he did not make clear exactly what had occurred, although it had something to do with rendering tallow on a "pila," from where it had been taken to *Kinki,* at San Pedro.

One result of the secularization of the Missions was an attack by hostile Indians from the desert on the buildings of the San Gabriel Mission's Rancho San Bernardino. Ornaments and vessels were taken from the chapel and grain from storage. Father Esténega journeyed there from San Gabriel, only to be captured and actually held prisoner for a while. Later several of the loyal Indians of the neighborhood were killed, so that a general exodus to San Gabriel was begun. Antonio Lugo's sons, who received Rancho San Bernardino from the governor, were harassed by bands of cattle thieves, some from quite distant tribes, and the history of this frontier abounds in action typical of the Wild West of fiction.

Mission San Fernando Rey was leased by Governor Pio Pico to his brother, and sold outright to Eulogio Celis in 1846. The outlying ranches of this Mission were parceled out to various individuals, but here resentment was expressed by the "neophytes," who seemed to be more aware of their own dispossession.

In 1844 Hugo Reid was elected to the position of "juez de paz," or justice of the peace, by the townspeople of San Gabriel. As he wrote in his "letters," those were troubled days. The Mexican citizens wanted a pueblo to be set up for the Indians, and the religious authority limited to a parish, which would clear the way to a distribution of the Mission lands. The move failed, largely because debts had piled up against the Mission and no one could see who would assume them or who would support a parish priest.

The local Indians became terrified because of irresponsible threats to reduce them to actual slavery. They turned more and more to drink and violence, the latter evil apparently attributable more to the Sonoran immigrants, or to the inroads of outlying tribesmen raiding for beef and horses, than to the remnant of the Gabrielinos in their little homes under the shadow of the Mission church.

Reid was at times forced to bring in soldiers to keep order in the town. He did call attention, however, to the fact that the great depredations were largely the work of raiders from beyond the mountain passes, and expeditions to quell the unruly invaders were organized.

In June, 1846, Reid and William Workman made arrangements to purchase the Mission, to assume the debts and the support of the padre. It may be that they felt they could better protect the local Indians in this way. But the sale was never actually carried to a conclusion due to the arrival of the North Americans, who formulated a policy of restoring the Mission churches and small acreages surrounding them to the Catholic Church. Thus, at the last, the Mission establishments were transformed into parish churches and prospered or failed to prosper as local conditions varied. Some of them were already so deteriorated as to be little more than ruins; others reached that status after continuing years of neglect. Restorations have sometimes been accomplished, fortunately, through the efforts of organizations or individuals interested in preserving the historical buildings of California.

The period between the secularization of the Missions and the coming of the North Americans was one of political strife between factions of the Mexican settlers and of demoralization for the Indians. Reid wrote of the situation as it had been in 1844, "The different missions had alcaldes continually on the move, hunting them up and carrying them back, but to no purpose: it was labor in vain." Many Gabrielinos went as far north as Monterey, he reported, while Indians from the counties to the south filled "the Angeles and surrounding ranchos with more servants than were required. Labor was in consequence very cheap."

To add to the confusion additional immigrants from Sonora, in Mexico, began to overrun the countryside. To continue with Reid's account: "They invaded the *rancheria*, gambled with the men, and taught them to steal: they taught the women to be worse than they were, and the men and women both to drink. Now we do not mean or pretend to say that the neophytes were not previous to this addicted to both drinking and gaming, with an inclination to steal, while under the domination of the church: but the Sonoreños most certainly brought them to a pitch of licentiousness before unparalleled in their history."

The treaty of Guadalupe Hidalgo, ratified by the United States in May of 1848, officially ended the Mexican War and certified the claim of the United States to California. The Gabrielinos, who spoke a Spanish still highly flavored with their Shoshonean accent, were now supposed to learn English and a whole new code of customs and attitudes.

For 77 years these Indians had been deprived of the use of their own tribal organization and group initiative in a rigid conformity to the direction of alien rules. Thoroughly confused by the spasmodic relaxation and tightening of this control, the survivors turned more and more to that successor of the warming Mission wines, the "agua ardiente," the fiery water of grape brandy. They sensed at once that among the newcomers there was to be far less of the alternately harsh and indulgent paternalism of the old regime and far more of a galling contempt and indifference. Their only possible defense was to maintain for the most part a front of stolid silence, behind which ran a play of comment in which every weakness of the newcomers received a treatment varying from gentle irony to sharp satire. Toward evidences of goodwill the response was loyalty, expressed in faithful service.

In the later 1850s San Gabriel settled down a bit.

Mrs. King described the town as she remembered it in that period. A long roadway led north from the Mission along the irrigation ditch to a vanishing point among the great live-oaks. The thatched adobe homes of the Indians who still clung to the Mission and to the fatherly concern of the priest were surrounded by little fields of corn, pumpkins, peas and chiles. Flowers "of the brightest hues nodded to their reflections in the rippling zanja." Shoshonean *Sibangna* had become the typical "sleepy Mexican village." The changes of the century looming ahead were to be far more startling, but the Gabrielinos were to have but a fragmentary and tragic share in them. A very short chapter remained in their history as members of a distinct tribe of American Indians.

Epilogue

$\mathbf{A}$ny account dealing with the last years of the Gabrielino Indians must lean heavily on the research of W. W. Robinson. His definitive work, "The Indians of Los Angeles: Story of the Liquidation of a People," was published by Glen Dawson of Los Angeles, the eighth of the "Early California Travel Series." Packed into 36 pages, one finds here both the statistics and drama of the episodes during which the last hope for the continuance of these people as a tribe, or as surviving individuals, was crushed.

As Robinson makes clear, the cluster of huts which stood between the orchards of Juan Domingo and one Sanchez bore no relation to the original *Yangna*. Where that had spread from hill to river now lay Los Angeles. officially since 1835 a "ciudad," or city, but still called the Pueblo, the town. The segregated district to which the Indians of the community were moved in 1836 lay

One of the last Mission Indian jacales in San Gabriel. (Security First National Bank collection).

near the southeast corner of the present Commercial and Alameda Streets and was called by the townfolk the "Rancheria of the Poblanos."

Some of the inhabitants of the ramshackle "jacales" of the rancheria may have been descendants of the original *Yavitam*, but for the most part they were of a polyglot origin. With the secularization of the Missions a great shift of population had occurred. Gabrielinos scattered in every direction, mostly to the north, and Indians from San Diego and San Luis Rey moved into Los Angeles. Only the whispered tales of his elders would have told a child of the Missions which village had been the home of his ancestors or where it had stood, and now the bewildered and uprooted folk wandered about with little sense of tribal or village origins. The next generation would find their surviving descendants absorbed into other tribes or other racial strains, their own identities for the most part quite lost.

The ragged folk from the rancheria continued to receive pittances for menial tasks. Labor in the vineyards was often paid in the form of "aguardiente," and those who possessed a few coins found every other door in the back streets of the Pueblo open to them as an informal "cantina" where this potent grape brandy could be purchased.

Quite regularly of a Saturday night many of the aborigines who lived in the rancheria, or who could reach it from the countryside, roamed the streets of the Pueblo in some stage of intoxication. It became necessary to round them up and confine them in a sort of open corral, from which on Monday morning they were released to return to their employment. All who were clearly vagrant found themselves working out fines, making repairs on the Pueblo church by the plaza or mending breaks in the "zanja madre," the "mother ditch," which brought water from the river for the domestic needs of the citizens and for irrigation of fields and vineyards.

More and more the "rancheria of the poblanos" became a source of worry and irritation to the Pueblo. The Indians were, as the Council admitted, "accustomed to bathe for their health," and they saw nothing wrong in a cleansing plunge in the "zanja madre." An edict was sent out forbidding this, and bathing in the river as well, unless the place chosen was well below the intake of the ditch. This seems reasonable to the 20th Century mind but it smacked a bit of discrimination on the part of those townsmen who were wont to divert the water around behind their own willow fences for domestic use before allowing it to proceed to homes and fields below.

Juan Domingo, that Johann Groningen who had acquired a wife from among the "gente de razon," a Mexican name and a fine vineyard, thought the time had come to annex a bit of land from the rancheria. The fence he built while carrying out this impulse was ordered torn down and he was fined; but in 1845 sentiment for eviction of the Indians had reached the point at which he was able to buy the site of the rancheria for 200 dollars. This, by coincidence, was the sum which Governor Pio Pico needed to defray the expenses of a trip north.

The new rancheria lay on the heights across the river. This place rejoiced in the title of "Pueblito" and had a short and hectic career of only two years before it was leveled to the ground. During its heyday the American period began and Pueblito held a lethal fascination for the United States soldiers of the garrison left in Los Angeles when Commodore Stockton went on to Monterey. Even after the Indian village was declared out-of-bounds it remained a sore spot, and its bad reputation could only be erased by its complete annihilation.

"From then on employers of Indian servants were to be responsible for their shelter and care," wrote Robinson. "Cooks and house-servants could run errands but had to keep off the streets after vespers. Self-employed Indians were to stay outside the city limits and in widely separated localities. Unemployed Indians were to be assigned to public works or to jail. The sum of $24 was collected to compensate Indians forced to move their huts from Pueblito."

Keeping to themselves, quiet and aloof, were a few families of islanders, the *Pipimares*, who lived in four huts to the south of the rancheria. Pressure was brought to have them join the other Indians in Pueblito or to have their employers offer housing. The record is silent as to what became of them and this would seem to be the last time they are mentioned as a living people. The great artisans and fishermen of the Channel Islands, the religious innovators for whom the mainlanders had felt such veneration, thus disappeared in a lasting silence.

The Mexican Californians had no active dislike of Indians. Though they dealt with them in no spirit of equality, kept them segregated in dwellings, church services and burial places, and dealt out heavy punishments for comparatively slight offenses, they professed an indulgent regard for them as patient servants and amiable, if erring, children. Some of the North American settlers adopted this attitude, as they did many of the attitudes and customs of the "Paisanos" among whom they settled in those early days of the American period, but others never looked at a California Indian with any other feeling than contempt.

The typical pioneer had fought his way across the continent, as S. F. Cook points out, "in bloody wars with strong, determined red-skins." The California tribes, as seen in the northern mining country, shy, wild seed-gatherers, comparatively peaceful, appeared to these vigorous newcomers as utterly deficient in any quality which could command respect.

In the south this opinion was confirmed. In the hungry, ill and often drunken Indians roaming the streets of the Pueblo of Los Angeles no one bothered to see the fine, if still primitive, characteristics which lay beneath the rags. In the north an actual war of extermination was fought. One writer described this as a "war against rabbits," insofar as relative strength was concerned. It helped ease what consciences the newcomers possessed to lump all of the California Indians under the epithet of "Diggers," and to repeat until it became a truism still echoed in our own time that all were alike degenerate and little above the animal in intelligence. When California became a state it was written into the law that no Indian could testify in court, even in his own defense.

On the North Americans the life of the Pueblo and of the ranchos in the country roundabout, one of leisurely pace and easy hospitality, had a strong influence. It was, in large measure, gratefully adopted as their own. That this life was based on Indian service and would join many a greater civilization of the past in oblivion, once that source of practically free labor had been destroyed, they seemed to comprehend as little as did the "Paisanos," the "people of the land."

In the memoirs of one early settler we catch a
glimpse of the economy of the 1860s when the great
vineyards, planted largely from the parent stock of the
Mission grapes, were in their heydey. The writer gave
this picture: "There were no wine presses and the
grapes were placed in huge shallow vats placed near
the 'sanja' or water ditch. The Indians were made to
bathe their feet in the sanja and then step into the vats
where they trod rhythmically up and down in the
grapes to press out the juice. Quite a number of Indians
were in the vat at one time. The juice was drained off
into larger vats where it was left to stand until fermentation. Then it was clarified, aged and bottled or bar-
reled.

"We all enjoyed drinking the pale red grape juice
when it had stood just a day or two before it began to
ferment. During the process of fermentation it was extremely intoxicating."

The problem of drunken Indians vexed the officials
of the new regime as it had the alcaldes of the decade
before the coming of the North Americans. On Monday mornings the open-air jail contained many a faithful worker sleeping off the dire effects of his Saturday
night "salary." Sheer numbers precluded the finding of
enough jobs on the public works to pay fines, as had
been the custom.

On August 16, 1860, the Council came up with a
solution in the form of an ordinance which read,
"When the city has no work in which to employ the
chain gang, the Recorder shall, by means of notices
conspicuously posted, notify the public that such a
number of prisoners will be auctioned off to the highest bidder for private service, and in that manner
they shall be disposed of for a sum which shall not
be less than the amount of their fine for double the
time they were to serve at hard labor."

The net effect of this ordinance, W. W. Robinson
observes, was the establishment of a veritable slave
market. Vineyardists and other employers were on
hand on Monday mornings to bid for the services of
the released prisoners. The amounts averaged from one

to three dollars for each Indian for a week's work. On Saturday night one third of the fee was paid to the Indian, often in the form of "aguardiente," and the balance went in cash into the treasury of Los Angeles. Horace Bell said of this practice, "Thousands of honest, useful people were utterly destroyed in this way." Robinson estimates the survival of individuals caught in this tragic cycle as limited to three years at the maximum.

J. Ross Browne, a native of Dublin, who was appointed in 1855 to be Customs Official and Inspector of Indian Affairs on the Pacific Coast, left such brilliant and satirical comments on the plight of the aborigines he visited that his works present a temptation to quote pages rather than paragraphs. Of the situation in the Pueblo he wrote, "The inhabitants of Los Angeles are a moral and intelligent people, and many of them disapprove of the custom on principle, and hope it will be abolished as soon as the Indians are all killed off. Practically, it is not a bad way of bettering their condition: for some of them die every week from the effects of debauchery, or kill one another in the nocturnal brawls which prevail on the outskirts of the Pueblo."

Laura Evertsen King described the passing of "Tintin" of San Gabriel, which might stand as a symbol of the closing years of his people and of "romantic California" as well, since without the Indian it became necessary for "Paisanos" of any origin to take the Indian's burden on their own backs or starve. Mrs. King wrote of "Tin-tin:" "All the week he labored faithfully and conscientiously, but on Sunday morning he would be seen by those on their way to church with his head in the ditch, dragged there by some friend, to cool him off for Monday's work. He was a fine specimen of the Indian, as he was, and could be but for the civilization of the white man, being tall and straight, and well built. But what constitution could stand 'fire water' and exposure week after week? In his prime he was taken from the ditch for the last time, a victim of his appetite, and the greed of the white man."

From the extreme simplicity of the early Mission pe-

Old Rojerio was a silversmith and sang in the San Fernando
Mission choir. (Photo taken in 1898 by C. C. Pierce).

riod the standard of living of the Californians had risen
to something more luxurious. With the coming of the
North Americans new sources of cash income developed. Beef delivered on the hoof at the mines was one
of these. Yet the dwindling of the Indian labor supply,
the droughts of the early '60s, the love of indolence and
good living, and in some cases the expense of defending

— 183 —

title to land before the United States Land Commission spelled downfall to many of the rancheros.

Debts acquired to help a man continue in his customary style over what was expected to be a temporary difficulty were found to be pyramiding, due to ruinous interest. Foreclosures were indecently swift. Either through sales or through disaster, many of the ranchos fell into strange hands. sometimes before the original titles were confirmed. In less than a century the oak groves and grasslands of the Gabrielinos had passed, for the most part, from the ownership of the descendants of the first Europeans to occupy them.

Under the new regime Fourth of July was celebrated in Los Angeles in great style, at least until the Civil War divided neighbor from neighbor. On these occasions the oratory was brilliant, the ladies' gowns of fashion's latest, the drinks most potent. Men raced up and down the streets on horseback, kicking up a tremendous dust and firing guns, very drunk and gay. No one arrested them or asked them to work off fines in the vineyards, while on the outskirts of the crowd ragged Indians watched the excitement in wondering silence.

In the '50s and '60s there yet remained an opportunity to rescue and rehabilitate the surviving Gabrielinos and the miscellaneous tribesmen who had drifted into the circle of their ancient boundaries to share their fate. Hugo Reid, although the best informed, was not the only man interested in justice, nor the only correspondent of the "Los Angeles Star."

We are indebted to John Walton Caughey for research which has brought to light quotations from early letters, such as one appearing in the issue of December 3, 1853, the writer of which put in a good word for the disposition of the Indians. He wrote, "Now we have no heart to do the Marshall the slightest prejudice, but this leading off of Indians and locking them up at night, for the purpose of taking away their paltry dollars, seems to us a questionable act: especially as they are seldom quarrelsome: and, more especially, as, unlike some white men whom the Marshall is too discreet

Dolphin carved from steatite by Gabrielino Indians.

to arrest: they do not, when drunk, brandish knives and pistols through the streets, threatening the safety of quiet citizens."

In 1852 another letter to the "Star" commented on the reduction by the House of Representatives of a proposed appropriation of $120,000 for the relief of the California Indians to a mere $20,000. The writer pointed out the sources of food and livelihood which had been taken over for the mining and agriculture of the white man, the starving conditions of the original owners from whose lands were then being exported 60 millions in gold annually, while from one port alone the Treasury received a yearly revenue of $3,000,000. This writer concluded, "If this be the policy of this government toward this people, it will form a dark page of history, if it does not bring the vengeance of heaven upon us as a nation."

The report of Benjamin D. Wilson on "The Indians of Southern California," written in 1852, was made available on its hundredth anniversary by the editing of J. W. Caughey for its publication by the Huntington Library. It brings to attention another champion of the Indians, one who should not be forgotten. Caughey's inclusion of biographical material has given a picture of this early settler which highlights his directness and simplicity.

Though "Don Benito's" biography reads like good Western fiction, replete with trapping and fur trading in early New Mexico and expeditions after the desert Indian marauders of the ranchos in Southern California, it was only when the gold rush brought miners hungry for beef into the northern counties that the energetic merchant and ranchero became the wealthy Mr. Wilson. Good fortune did not change him. He could trail Indian cattle thieves into the wildest country, give wounds and receive them, but always he retained a feeling for Indians as human beings and individuals. They felt his man-to-man understanding and gave him their confidence to a rare degree. In his grandson, General George S. Patton, more recent history records many of his qualities of courage.

Wilson could see only one solution of the "Indian Problem" of California, a system of reservations. He was appointed to the modest post of sub-agent under Edward F. Beale. This brilliant and energetic army officer was appointed in 1852 to be superintendent of Indian Affairs for California. No effort was too great for these two men, Wilson and Beale, as they looked forward to carrying out a plan which they hoped would contain the best features of the Mission system, but with a definite view of placing well-trained Indians with restored hope and initiative on land which would support them adequately and be their own forever.

Wilson immediately went to work compiling his voluminous report on the condition of the Indians of Southern California. He quoted Hugo Reid in his use of the term "Gabrielino," but so greatly had the tribe diminished that Wilson himself seemed to lump the local Indians as one with the Luiseños, listing only the Cahuilla and the Serrano as distinct tribes. From a manuscript of Reid's which Wilson saw he copied a description of the San Gabriel and San Fernando Indians which pictured them as of "pleasing countenance, well-formed features, and in many cases of a light complexion, which is not caused by a mixture of blood."

Wilson envisioned a reservation for Indians which took in the larger part of the desert regions from Santa

Isabela Rancho in San Diego county, all the way through Temecula and ranchos known by the names of San Jacinto and San Gorgonio to Tejon, and on to Four Creeks in the Tulare country. It was land of no appeal to white settlers of the middle 19th century, but it contained many a spring and patch of fertile land where an Indian could have found a livelihood.

On land near Tejon, south of Bakersfield, which was actually set aside Beale started a pilot reservation. More than a thousand Indians of a number of tribal ancestries came there on the 12th of September in 1852. To them the plan was outlined, with Wilson interpreting in Spanish. In February of the next year Beale reported that they were working steadily, without complaint, and as the fruits of their labor began to appear, with delight. His own feelings, he said, had at first been merely of compassion but were changing into "a deep interest in their welfare, and in many instances to a personal attachment." Again he wrote, "I have no military force here, and require none; my door has neither been locked nor barred night or day, and yet my feeling of security is as great as though I were surrounded by an armed guard."

Caughey quoted the statistics which lay behind Beale's enthusiasm. Twenty-five hundred Indians had planted 2600 acres in wheat, barley and corn, and were setting up irrigation systems. The first crop was reported at 42,000 bushels of wheat and 10,000 of barley. An article in the "Los Angeles Star" on June 24, 1854, praised the result which had been obtained so early and said of Beale, "Let him have a fair trial and he will make the wild Indians of California the happiest people in the State."

Beale was not to be allowed this fair trial. The office of sub-agent in which Wilson labored so devotedly was abolished a year after it was set up, and in the summer of 1854 Beale was removed from office and made to face charges of misuse of funds. He was later able to prove his innocence, but the experiment lay in ruins.

Not only had Wilson's recommendation for ample reservations to be set aside in the desert areas been ignored, but actual treaties—18 of them, negotiated with good sense and careful study by three men appointed as commissioner-agents for this purpose—failed of ratification in Washington. The hope which had been inspired by the treaty conferences was shown to be futile. The Gabrielinos, already negligible in numbers, had not figured in the treaty negotiations as a tribe and it would be difficult to ascertain whether any of them had been among the farmers of Tejon, under Beale; yet it is probable that not a few of the descendants of Mission Indians had joined the "wild" tribesmen in this experiment.

Mission Indian girl. (Photo taken in 1941 by Bertha P. Cody).

In 1867 the time had come for the community of Los Angeles to throw off the pleasant lethargy it had inherited from the preceding century. Letters to the "Star" made tentative suggestions toward the establishment of a system of garbage collection, as against the time-honored custom of throwing refuse into the street for the dogs and visiting sea-gulls to remove. A system of water distribution was installed, consisting of pipes made from hollowed logs. The town began to turn its face away from the old Plaza, now graced by a new brick reservoir, and to dream of a future as an American city.

Miss Mary Foy, whose memories fill many a gap in

local history, looked back upon the coming of iron pipes, in place of the wooden ones which proved inefficient, as the crucial moment of transition when the Pueblo ceased to exist and the future metropolis was born. This seems a valid suggestion, so that 1867, when a contract was awarded for the laying of the first iron pipes, may be as good a date as any to mark the end of a century in which the Gabrielino Indians had made a brave but losing effort to adapt to the ways of a succession of alien rulers.

Yangna, and her numerous sister rancherias, had become nothing more than archeological sites. When the Bella Union Hotel was rebuilt in 1870 Gabrielino game-stones were unearthed among many other artifacts. No one could think of a use for them although there were still a few Indians, living in scattered shanties or employed on ranches, who could have explained the rules of the old games. A few individuals still emerged from obscurity to do laundry for the gentry, or to carry water in ollas hung from shoulder yokes whenever the pipes failed or the intakes were washed out in the winter floods.

The "Indian Problem" continued to vex the people of California, but what remained for the few surviving Gabrielinos was only an epilogue. This was uttered for them by one of John Peabody Harrington's aged informants, when early in the 20th Century he spoke some of the last syllables any one was ever to hear in the ancient Shoshonean dialect of the region: *"Wi-kumimuk taraxat we,"* "When Indians died, the villages ended," he explained. "We, all the people, ended."

Suggested Additional Reading

BENEDICT, RUTH F.
    1924   A Brief Sketch of Serrano Culture. *American Anthropologist*, vol. 26: 366-392. Menasha.

BOLTON, HERBERT E.
    1927   *Fray Juan Crespi, Missionary Explorer on the Pacific Coast, 1769-1774.* (Crespi's diary). Berkeley.

BOSCANA, FRAY GERÓNIMO
    1933   *Chinigchinich.* (Tr. by Alfred Robinson; annotations by J. P. Harrington; foreword by F. W. Hodge; ed. by Phil T. Hanna). Santa Ana.

BROWNE, JOHN ROSS
    1944   *The Indians of California.* (Reprint). San Francisco.

COOK, SHERBURNE F.
    1955   The Conflict Between the California Indian and White Civilization. University of California, *Ibero-Americana*: 21-24. Berkeley and Los Angeles.

HEMERT-ENGERT, A. VAN, & TEGGART, F. J. (EDS.)
    1910   The Narrative of the Portolá Expedition of 1769-1770 by Miguel Costansó. Academy of Pacific Coast History, *Publications*, vol. 1, no. 4. Berkeley.

KROEBER, ALFRED L.
    1953   *Handbook of the Indians of California.* (2nd edition). Berkeley.

MACGOWAN, KENNETH
    1950   *Early Man in the New World.* New York.

PALÓU, FRAY FRANCISCO
    1934   *The Expedition into California of the Venerable Fray Junípero Serra and His Companions in the Year 1769.* (Tr. and arr. by Douglas S. Watson and Thomas W. Temple II). San Francisco.

REID, HUGO
    1926   *The Indians of Los Angeles County.* (Reprinted from his letters on "Angeles County Indians" in the *Los Angeles Star*). Los Angeles.

Robinson, Wm. W.
 1939   *Ranchos Become Cities.* Pasadena.
 1948   *Land in California.* Berkeley and Los Angeles.
 1952   *The Indians of Los Angeles.* Los Angeles.

Rogers, David B.
 1929   *Prehistoric Man of the Santa Barbara Coast.* Santa Barbara.

Shinn, Geo. H.
 1941   *Shoshonean Days.* Glendale.

Strong, Wm. D.
 1929   Aboriginal Society in Southern California. University of California, *Publications in American Archaeology and Ethnology,* vol. 26. Berkeley.

Smith, D. E., & Teggart, F. J. (Eds.)
 1909   Diary of Gaspar de Portolá During the California Expedition of 1769-1770. Academy of Pacific Coast History, *Publications,* vol. 1, no. 3. Berkeley.

Wagner, Henry R.
 1924   *Juan Rodríguez Cabrillo.* Berkeley.

Walker, Edwin F.
 1951   Five Prehistoric Archeological Sites in Los Angeles County, California. Southwest Museum, *Hodge Anniversary Publications,* vol. VI. Los Angeles.

A comprehensive bibliography of the Gabrielino Indians, in manuscript form, is on file in the Southwest Museum Library.

Index

A

Acagchemen (A-hash-amen), 40
Achoicomingna (Achois Comihabit), 125
Acurangna, 165, 166
Ahau (Aguai, Ahaungna), 85
Akvangna, 21
Alamitos Bay, 39, 40, 80, 85
Alarcón, Ensign, 97
Aleupkingna (Ahupkina, Aleupkig-na), 158, 159, 165
Aleuts, 102
Alliklik, 13, 127
Aliso Creek, 1, 37, 39, 86, 87, 116, 118
American Museum of Natural History, 110
Amupke, 20
Amutscupiabe (Amutscupiavit; also see Rancho Muscupiabe), 19, 20, 165
Angeles Mesa, 94
Anza, Juan Bautista de, 135
Apachia (Apatsijan), 123, 168
Arboretum, Los Angeles, 158, 161
Arcadia, 161
Arellano, Francisco de, 101
Arrowhead Springs, 20
Arroyo Seco, 120, 145ff, 163ff
Arts and Crafts, 14, 16, 32
Asawtngna, 12
Asención, Fr. Antonio de la, 97, 101, 131
Asuksangna (Asuesabit), 1, 144
Ataviangna, 89
Avalon, 99, 106
Awingna (Aguibit, Ahuingna, Ahujvit, Ajuenga, Ajuinga, Ajuivit, Awig-na, Ouiichi), 142, 143
Axaxa (Axawkngna, Paxauxa), 35, 36
Azusa, 78

B

Bakersfield, 13
Baldwin, Elias J., 158
Baldwin Hills, 77, 78
Ballona Creek (La Ballona), 78, 94, 123, 124
Bancroft, Hubert H., 87, 88
Barrows, H. D., 165
Bassett, 78, 120
Bay of Smokes, 87, 88
Beale, Edward F., 126, 186ff
Bear Mountain, 21
Bell, Horace, 182
Benedict, Ruth, 49, 140, 141
Beverly Hills, 77, 78, 124
Big Bear Lake, 41
Bixby (Flint, Bixby & Co.), 81
Bixby, Llewellyn, 82
Bixby Ranch, 39, 85
Bixby Slough, 89
Boats, 7, 8
Bolsa Chica, 87
Bolton, Herbert E., 123
Boscana, Fr. Gerónimo, 23ff, 37, 47ff, 83, 94, 106, 133
Boschke's Island, 90
Bowers, Stephen, 110
Boys' Initiation (Toloache Ceremony), 57ff, 133
Brainerd, George W., 91
Brea Canyon, 118
Brea Pits (Tar Pits), 94
Browne, J. Ross, 182
Bryan, Bruce, 110
Burnham, W. M., 107

C

Cabrillo, Juan Rodríguez, 87, 88, 97ff, 136
Cabuepet (see Kawengna)
Cahuenga, 9, 10, 127
Cahuilla, 6ff, 23, 36, 47ff
Cajon Pass, 3, 14, 19
Calabasas (Calabzas), 11
Camarillo, 127